Zen Heart, Zen Mind

Zen Master **AMA Samy** (Gen-Un-Ken) is the only Indian so far to have received the Dharma Seal of Enlightenment from a recognized Zen master. Born Arul Maria Arokiasamy in 1936, AMA Samy joined the Jesuit order after finishing school and became a priest. In 1972, he went to Japan to train in Zen under Yamada Ko-Un Roshi. He began teaching Zen in the eighties and, in 1996, established the Zen centre, Bodhi Zendo, at Perumalmalai, Kodaikanal, where he lives and teaches.

A student of Zen Master AMA Samy, **Sridevi Rao** has been a professional writer and editor for over 15 years, working in various capacities with periodicals, journals and newspapers. She currently runs a design agency in Chennai, specializing in corporate communications.

ZEN HEART, ZEN MIND
THE TEACHINGS OF ZEN MASTER AMA SAMY

Compiled and edited by
Sridevi Rao

Cre-A:

ISBN 81-85602-81-6

First Edition April 2002

Published by
Cre-A:
New No 2, 24th East Street
Thiruvanmiyur, Chennai 600 041
e-mail : crea@vsnl.com

Printed at Sudarsan Graphics, Chennai 600 017

© AMA Samy

Distributed by
EastWest Books (Madras) Pvt. Ltd.

Karmaveerar Kamaraj Bhavan
No 571 (Old No. 327 & 328)
Poonamallee High Road
Aminjikarai
Chennai 600 029

3-5-1108
Maruti Complex
II Floor
Narayanaguda
Hyderabad 500 029

I Floor
Praja Bhavan
53/2 Bull Temple Road
Basavangudi
Bangalore 560 019

Editor's Note 7
About Master Ama Samy 9
Preface 12

The Zen Method

Zazen: The Buddha Sits 21
Shikantaza: The *Zazen* of Intimacy 32
The *Zazen* of Equanimity, Joy and Compassion 37
Koan Zen: The Questing Heart-Mind 43

Teisho

Part I Your Original Face

Your Original Face Before You Were Born 56
Snow Heaped in a Silver Bowl 68
Coming Home 76
Thousand Mistakes, Ten Thousand Mistakes 83
Unmon and the Sickness of the World 91
Child of Emptiness 99

Part II If Not Now, When?

If Not Now, When? 110
Heart Broken, Heart of Love 117

The Way of the Heart-Mind 127
Everyday Mind is the Way 135

Awakening

Mountains are not Mountains, Rivers are not Rivers 151
Not One, Not Two 159
Mountains are Mountains, Rivers are Rivers 165

A Brief History of Zen 174

List of Reading Material 193

Editor's Note

Most of the content of this volume has been culled from various talks given by Zen Master AMA Samy to his students. Where necessary, it has been reworked by Master AMA Samy and the editor to suit this publication. The section on Awakening has been put together from earlier writings of the Master.

A Zen talk or *teisho* or dharma talk is quite unlike any other. Sometimes refreshingly simple and direct, sometimes highly elliptical and metaphorical, sometimes sharp and concise, sometimes leisurely and rambling, it seeks to cut through the habitual patterns of reason and logic, and speaks directly to the heart-mind of the listener. Passages (especially some of the *koans* that pepper the talks) may seem incomprehensible on a first reading, but they stay somewhere just below the consciousness, breaking through when we least expect it to give us a glimmer of understanding, an instant of what Zen practitioners love to call the 'Aha!' experience. The *teishos* in the book have been carefully selected to present, as far as possible, the full flavour of Master AMA Samy's teachings. Of course, the written word does not always convey the inner silences that inform the Master's spoken word and manner to give *teishos* their full import. Layered with many levels of meaning, they are best read—or savoured, rather—slowly, repeatedly and open-mindedly. Then, all at once, they seem as alive, as fresh and vital as, to use a phrase of Master AMA Samy, the falling flower, and the morning dew.

Liberty has been taken in using either the Chinese or Japanese names of Zen masters, whichever is better known, in the book. For example, Master Joshu is better known by the Japanese version of his name rather than by the Chinese original, Chao-Chou, and therefore the former has been used.

Sridevi Rao

About Master AMA Samy

Zen Master AMA Samy (Gen-Un-Ken) is the only Indian so far to have received the Dharma Seal of Enlightenment from a recognized Zen master.

Born Arul Maria Arokiasamy of Indian Christian parents in Burma in 1936, AMA Samy came to India after the War. Driven by poverty, his parents put him in the care of his maternal grandfather, a devotee of a Muslim saint, who considered it his sacred duty to tend the burial shrine of the saint. The grandfather died soon after in an accident, leaving the young boy without support and guidance. However, the boy managed to finish school and joined the Jesuit order.

In course of time, AMA Samy became a priest, but his heart was still restless for god. "During my Jesuit training and studies my spiritual life became quite empty and lost," he has said. "I had come seeking liberation and god-experience but I did not find them." He turned to the Upanishads and they opened up his heart and mind. He began visiting Hindu ashrams, but while they inspired him they failed to give him what he sought. Then he met the ascetic Swami Abhishiktananda and became eager to follow him as a homeless mendicant. Abhishiktananda did not encourage him on that path, and introduced him instead to the teachings of the south Indian Advaitic sage Ramana Maharshi. Moved by Ramana's vision, AMA Samy devoted himself to finding the answer to the question the great sage poses: *Who Am I?* For a while, he was a wandering mendicant but eventually settled down as a hermit near a holy shrine in Dindigul district, where the village people fed him. He suffered many privations but persisted in his quest and finally came to Awakening with the question that he had set himself.

He needed his Realization to be tested and authenticated, however, and around this time he fortuitously met Father Enomiya Lasalle, who not only introduced him to Zen but also helped him go to Japan to train under Yamada Ko-Un Roshi in Kamakura.

Yamada Ko-Un was the chief disciple of Yasutani Haku-Un Roshi who, in turn, was the disciple of Harada Dai-Un. Harada belonged to the Soto school of Zen, but he also trained in the Rinzai school of *koan* Zen. Harada's disciple Yasutani integrated *koan* Zen with the Soto approach of *zazen*, and Yamada Ko-Un continued this practice. Yasutani and Yamada together started the Sanbo Kyodan School, which was one of the first Zen schools in Japan to accept foreigners as students. (Yasutani Roshi's approach and teaching are detailed in the book *Three Pillars of Zen*, edited by Philip Kapleau. The book also carries an account of the *satori* or Enlightenment of Yamada Ko-Un, referred to as a businessman by the initials 'K.Y.')

Yamada Ko-Un confirmed AMA Samy's Awakening, after which AMA Samy completed the course of *koan* study under him to deepen his Realization. In 1982 he received authorization to teach from Yamada Ko-Un Roshi, who died in 1989. He also received the Dharma name Gen-Un-Ken, meaning Dark or Original Cloud, from his master.

AMA Samy began teaching Zen in the early eighties. In 1996, he established the Zen centre, Bodhi Zendo, at Perumalmalai, Kodaikanal. It offers Zen training year-round in both the Soto and Rinzai methods. The Bodhi Sangha (AMA Samy's community of students and disciples) is spread all over Europe, USA, Australia and, of course, India. AMA Samy spends a few months every year in travel abroad, teaching and helping his students.

The spiritual journey has also brought AMA Samy back full circle to the Christian tradition to which he belongs and to which he brings a fresh, eclectic approach. "I am often asked to what religion I owe my allegiance," he has said. "I stand in the in-between of Hinduism, Buddhism and Christianity." He stands true to Christ, true to Zen and true to the human heart-mind.

Editor

Bodhi Zendo can be reached at: Bodhi Zendo, Perumalmalai, Kodaikanal 624104
e-mail: mail@bodhizendo.org   URL: www.bodhizendo.org

Preface

When I first met my master, Yamada Ko-Un Roshi, in Kamakura, Japan, he said with a twinkle in his eyes, "I am so glad that Bodhidharma has at last come to see me!" When I finished my *koan* curriculum with him and was leaving, he said, "Japan is known for importing things, making them better and then exporting them. So now I am exporting Zen back to India!"

Zen has its roots in India, in the *dhyana* tradition of Mahayana Buddhism. It was received as Ch'an in China, where it took the particular form and style that came to be known as Zen. Zen is the rare and marvellous udumbara flower in the garden of Buddhism. It is concrete, particular and experience-oriented. It is this-worldly and celebrates life and nature. It is oriented to the beautiful and the simple, it is centred in the Now, is sensitive to and appreciative of the finite and the mortal, the falling flower and the morning dew. It loves paradox and parable, is full of humour and laughter; it is mystical and compassionate.

In the West, Zen has often been portrayed as being individualistic and anarchic. We cannot deny that Zen is individualistic, but to portray this one feature as central to Zen is to misunderstand it. Zen straddles discipline and freedom, individuality and community, immanence and transcendence, reason and paradox. In short, Zen is both wisdom and compassion.

In practice, Zen has not been without its share of problems. Many so-called Enlightened masters leading dissipated lives have done great damage and harm to Zen schools and institutions, particularly in the West. That is why there is need for a critical Sangha, or community of practitioners, and for critical and authentic Enlightened masters.

Today Zen is known in India and books on Zen appear to be quite popular. But not so the practice of Zen. It is not an easy path—the discipline and committed training that Zen calls for is often arduous. Yet the fruits of this practice can be tasted in the here and now, not just in some after-life. Who among us has the *bodhicitta*, the heart-mind of Awakening, to give themselves wholeheartedly to the Dharma? Of course, unless one is called, one will not come; unless one is seeking, one will not hear the call. But unless the Dharma is 'preached' one will not hear. Thus, I offer these short pieces in service of the Dharma and as a help to seekers.

This book is a brief articulation of my vision and experience, a guide to my Dharma brothers and sisters on the Way. It is a finger pointing to the moon.

I am grateful to Sridevi Rao who has edited these pages. She has also added a chapter on the history of Zen. She has given much loving care and effort to this work and I am thankful to her. Dr T K Gopalan took keen interest in this work and offered valuable comments. Dr Meera Rajagopalan copy-edited the manuscript. S Ramakrishnan, the publisher, showed great care and sensitivity in bringing out this publication. I thank all of them.

AMA Samy

A Note from the Author and Editor

The form of the present text has grown out of not only the talks, but also numerous notes made by the author over the years. The notes were made out of personal interest and not specifically for use in the present context. Accurate indication of sources has therefore not been possible. The author acknowledges his indebtedness to these sources. However, a list of reading material has been included for general reference.

To study the Buddha way is to study the self;
To study the self is to forget the self;
To forget the self is to be Enlightened by
the ten thousand dharmas;
To be Enlightened by the ten thousand dharmas is to
remove the barrier between the self and the others;
No trace of Enlightenment remains, and this no-
trace continues endlessly.

— Dogen Kigen

"Seek not to follow in the footsteps of the Ancient One;
Seek what they sought"

The Zen Method

It is the peculiar nature of the Zen tradition that while the rules for sitting meditation—posture, breathing, the ritualistic bowing before and after, and so on—are very strict and formal to an extreme, they are rarely 'taught' to the individual student.

At Bodhi Zendo, Kodaikanal, as in most modern Zen centres, beginners are usually given a brief orientation—about enough not to disturb other practitioners by doing things out of turn—and then expected to learn as they go along. In the *zendo*, or Zen meditation hall, monitors ensure that postures are maintained (spine erect, knees on floor, hands joined on the lap) and apply the *kyosaku/keisaku* (a wooden paddle) to shoulders slumped in drowsiness or tiredness. This practice originates in the hard whacks administered by Zen masters in ancient times to jolt their disciples into Awakening, but in modern *zendos* it is used at fixed sitting periods during the day on the acupressure points on the shoulders to refresh the meditator. It is usually employed on request, conveyed by the meditator by joining her/his hands and holding them up.

Stringing together the practices and methods advocated by various Zen masters down the centuries, daily life at Bodhi Zendo includes periods of four hours of formal sitting meditation (*zazen*), *seva* or community activity, Zen Buddhist studies and formal one-on-one meetings or interviews (*dokusan/sanzen*) with the Master. *Sesshins*, lasting about a week, are times of intensive practice, with complete silence and over eight hours of *zazen* a day.

In line with the tradition of his master, Yamada Ko-Un Roshi, Master AMA Samy prescribes the practices of both the Soto and Rinzai schools of Zen, advising the practice of *shikantaza* or *koan* study depending on the personality and aspirations of the student.

Precisely defined and quickly learned are the physical requirements of formal 'sitting' but rather loosely enunciated and therefore more enigmatic is the 'mental' process of meditation. Zen talks of concentration, but clearly differentiates it from the 'mechanical' concentration of mantra meditation. It talks of 'cutting off the mind' but also exhorts you to be 'ever alert'. It demands Great Faith but also prescribes Great Doubt.

What, then, is the method, what the technique? Zen Master AMA Samy shies away from giving too many instructions, as they would lead to a mechanical practice of what he calls 'lifeless Zen'. Rather, he uses pointers, in the form of symbols and images, to right practice. The contents of the chapters in this section have been culled from talks delivered by the Master over a period of time, containing tips and words of gentle encouragement to students during *sesshins*. The intention of the editor is not to make it a *zazen* manual but to let the words act as guide to the practitioners on the Way.

Editor

Zazen:
The Buddha Sits

A non-Buddhist philosopher said to the Buddha, "I do not ask for words; I do not ask for non-words." The Buddha just sat there. The philosopher said admiringly, "The World Honoured One, with his great mercy, has blown away the clouds of my illusion and enabled me to enter the Way." And after making his bows, he took his leave.

Then Ananda asked the Buddha, "What did he realize, to admire you so much?" The World Honoured One replied, "A fine horse runs even at the shadow of the whip."

Zazen literally means formal sitting meditation. It is central to the Zen way in the sense that you use the insights and attitudes that are present in your *zazen* to inform your every action and prepare the ground for self-transformation. This is the real practice of Zen. It is living Zen.

The natural question follows: what are these insights and attitudes that you gain or express in *zazen*? What happens or is expected to happen during Zen meditation? Can you expect to see the light, enter a state of bliss, hear drums and trumpets and the song of angels?

To sit in *zazen* is to sit without any such expectations. There is nothing to hear but the clamour of your own desires. Nothing to feel but the weight of your own emotions. Nothing to see but the repetitive patterns of your own ego-self.

Yet, understand that it is only through this 'seeing' of your separate self, your desires and your emotions that you come to see into your True Self, your Original Face. And that, at the core, is what *zazen* is all about: to see into your True Self.

How do we practise this 'seeing' in *zazen*? Is there a method to be followed, a technique to be learned? These are questions asked not only by beginners but also by 'advanced' students who are sometimes suddenly seized by doubt and seem to have lost their way.

I have often been reproached for giving too few 'instructions' on how to sit. I do so with some reason. There is a great temptation to translate Zen practice into a technique, an automated, mechanical discipline of body and mind. Too much emphasis tends to be laid on effort and concentration, on a desperate striving for a breakthrough. This is lifeless Zen.

I, too, tell my students to follow the ancient techniques of correct sitting but not as an end in itself. Your sitting is a practice in letting-go, in the surrender of the self, in self-transformation.

At our Zen Centre our practice involves both just sitting (Japanese *shikantaza*) and *koan* practice. The rules for sitting are those that have been followed unchanged for centuries. Sit on a cushion with your legs crossed in either full lotus or half-lotus posture, making sure that your knees are touching your floor mat or floor cushion. If you find this position difficult to get into and maintain, take the kneeling position, with a cushion placed between the legs or by seating yourself on a specially designed bench. If you are physically unable to assume these postures you may sit on a stool or straight-backed chair.

Once you have settled yourself in your position, straighten yourself from the hip up to hold your spine erect, your head, shoulders and back in a straight line. Pay special attention to your shoulders. Don't pull yourself up from the shoulders; keep them relaxed. Your shoulders may tense or slump as your mind wanders during practice: notice this and gently correct your posture.

Hold your head up, as if you are supporting the sky, with the chin tucked slightly in. The eyes are partially closed, unfocused and looking down about three feet ahead of you. You can, of course, occasionally close your eyes when they become tired, but keep in mind that with eyes closed there would be a greater tendency to slip into a doze or get caught up in visual hallucinations.

Your hands are placed on your lap, close to your belly, with the palm of the left hand facing upwards and resting on the palm of the right hand. The tips of the thumbs touch lightly, forming an oval. The elbows jut very slightly forward. Hold your hands in this position lightly and easily, as if you are holding a precious egg, throughout the *zazen* period. Never let them slacken, as they are wont to when your mind wanders.

Turn your attention to your breathing. Consciously deepen your breathing to start with. Expand and contract your diaphragm as you inhale and exhale. Settle into the rhythm and then gently let go, not forcing the breath, just following it as it rises and falls, rises and falls.

Breath awareness is not just a beginner's practice—it is a lifelong practice. Focus on the sensations as the breath flows in and out. Follow the thread of your breath in your nostrils, at the back of your throat, in your chest, deep down in your belly. Become sensitive to the subtle sensations it causes at each stage of its journey from the tip of your nose to your belly and out again.

Breath counting is an equally effective practice, excellent for beginners and a lifeline for veterans who are suddenly and helplessly 'stuck' in their practice. As you inhale, count one: fix your attention unwaveringly on your breath. Exhale, resting your mind on the out-breath. Count two on your next inhalation. Finish one round at the count of ten and go back to one, this time counting your exhalations and resting on your inhalations. If your mind drifts away from your breath into daydreaming, bring it gently back to the breath, starting again from one. It is a simple practice but don't be surprised if you don't finish even one round in the initial days of your practice! Students have come to me in great anxiety about not getting past one in an entire period of sitting! These are the same students who have, in time, shown me that they go very deep in *zazen*.

Zen students, especially in the Japanese Zen monasteries, are told to 'drop the mind' into the *hara*, a region approximately four fingers below the navel, in *zazen*. This is a good centring practice, if done naturally. Don't force the breath into the *hara* or make strenuous efforts to focus on it. That would defeat the very purpose of your *zazen*. Just bring your awareness to the *hara* and hold it steady as you breathe in and out, in and out. Your mind is centred on the *hara* and at the same time it is wide open, abiding nowhere.

It is worth repeating that at no point should the breath be forced. Breathe normally. Especially don't force the breath deep into your abdomen. Keep the lower abdomen controlled but not tensed or contracted. I have noticed that it helps to consciously eliminate the fractional pause between inhalation and exhalation, exhalation and inhalation. It improves concentration.

Focus, attention, concentration—I use these words, but cautiously. Breath awareness is a centring, grounding practice.

Do not turn it into a mechanical technique. Rather, practise it as a form of non-doing; action in non-action.

When your breath flows evenly and naturally, your body relaxes into a rhythm and equilibrium. Your mind, which is not really separate from your body, dwells serenely in this state of natural balance and calm. This is why the method of following the breath that we practise in *zazen* is not a mechanical concentration technique but is a way of bringing your body-mind to oneness and openness.

Through breath awareness, the mind 'becomes' the body; the body-mind is then transcended or 'dropped' into unfocused, non-dual awareness. If I am to give a rule of thumb, it is this: if after *zazen* you feel exhausted, tired or restless your *zazen* was not good. Perhaps you were straining to concentrate, trying to achieve something or the other.

I am repeatedly asked how long each period of sitting should be. If you are practising on your own at home, I would say, go with what is comfortable for you. If you are a beginner, even ten minutes a day would be enough to start with. Don't set yourself too ambitious a target in the initial stages: your resolve will begin to falter if you encounter problems in sitting through prolonged periods of *zazen*. Instead, gradually increase the period of sitting.

I would also recommend that you allot yourself a fixed time everyday for *zazen*. Stick to it firmly, unless of course you are faced with a dire emergency. A renowned Zen practitioner once remarked that there are two types of Zen. First, there is kind and gentle Zen, that concedes you those occasional lapses in your routine, is understanding and sympathetic as you struggle to wake up in time for morning *zazen* and allows you to do it in your own time and at your own pace. This he calls 'grandmother Zen'. Then, there is the other type, that is firm to the point of sternness, hauls you up by the scruff of the neck every morning and plops you down on your *zazen* cushion. This, he says, is 'kickass Zen'. Which would you like to follow?

At our Zen centre, we intersperse sitting periods of 25 minutes each with *kinhin*, or walking meditation. This is a practice followed in Zen centres everywhere, though the duration of each period of sitting varies from centre to centre. We don't practise walking meditation just to give ourselves a break and a chance to stretch our legs as some people think. Walking meditation is an important part of Zen practice because it is meditation in action. Of course, in our everyday affairs we don't go about things at the pace at which we do *kinhin*, but the practice gives you a taste of breath-body-mind awareness in movement. You could make it part of your everyday practice, varying the speed with which you walk as you continue to practise awareness.

In our *zendo*, when the little bell that signifies the end of the sitting is sounded, we bring our hands together and bow down from the hip. Then we rise, bow once more and begin walking meditation. We fold the fingers of the right hand around the right thumb in a tight grasp and then hold the right hand lightly with the left hand. The hands are held thus in front of the chest, the forearms parallel to the floor. As we walk slowly around the *zendo*, we continue our practice: we are aware of our breath, aware of the movement of our legs and feet as we lift each foot, move it in space and place it gently again on the ground. Those who are working on *koans* continue to work on them as they practise *kinhin*.

I am yet to meet a Zen practitioner who has not, at some point or the other, struggled with pain in the legs during *zazen*. Don't change your position as soon as you begin to feel uncomfortable. Don't move even if the discomfort worsens. My Zen master, Yamada Ko-Un, used to say, "Pain in the legs is the taste of Zen." Don't fight the pain. Taste it. Don't tell yourself,

"Oh, the damn pain is starting again, now it is going to spoil my meditation…" Rather, say to yourself, "Aha, there is that old sensation. Let's take a closer look." Be the pain. Watch it, focus your attention on it. You will notice that the pain never seems to stay in one spot very long. In fact, as soon as you turn your attention to it, it moves away to another spot. Continue focusing your attention on the pain and you will gradually find yourself less and less bothered by it. Of course, if you feel the pain is becoming unbearable, or if you feel a sharp shooting pain, shift your position to ease it. If your legs go to sleep adjust your posture a little. But try to push yourself a little each time in enduring the discomfort.

Come back to your breath, in the realization that it is not so much you who breathe in and out, it is the universe that breathes in and out. In the life-giving breath, all living beings and even non-sentient beings are united and bound together. When you are seated and are breathing, it is the universe that is seated and is breathing.

Zazen means coming back, over and over again, to your body-breath. Mind wanders, thoughts crowd in—pay them due attention, don't engage yourself in their drama but watch them as a disinterested observer, and come back to awareness of your breath. Over and over again. Zen Master Dogen calls it "exertion without end".

Random thoughts are the flotsam and jetsam of your consciousness; rest in your breath and let them float by. Your mindwaves are like the surface of the ocean, ever in motion; in *zazen*, you abide in the depths, in the centre of your being, in awareness and stillness.

Your consciousness is limitless, like the space in which clouds float, birds fly, rain falls. Images, thoughts, emotions are like the clouds, the birds, the rain that swirl in the vast space of your consciousness. Don't try to stop them. Let them come, let them go.

Zazen is being aware of awareness, consciousness becoming conscious of itself. It is a process of 'at-one-ing' with one's self, of realizing I AM. This consciousness-becoming-conscious is non-dual consciousness and is grounded in body awareness. Your body is more than your body. Your body-as-consciousness is openness to all reality; indeed the universe is the body. Be grounded in body awareness, in breath awareness in particular. Come again and again to the body-breath awareness. It is the universe actualizing its being as non-dual consciousness.

The great master of *zazen*, Dogen Kigen, wrote: "After the bodily position is in order, also regulate your breathing. If a thought arises, take note of it and then dismiss it. When you forget all attachments steadfastly, you will become *zazen* itself naturally. This is the art of *zazen*... the Dharma gate of great repose and joy."

In *zazen*, you are in the mode of not-knowing, not-thinking, not-wanting, not-seeking, not-acting. It is letting yourself be in *non-thinking*, which is neither thinking nor not-thinking: it is being in unknowing, in darkness, in mystery. It is a sort of resting, "abiding where there is no abiding", in deep faith, trust and surrender.

> *Master Yakusan was sitting in deep meditation when a monk came up to him and asked, "Solidly seated as a rock, what are you thinking?"*
>
> *The master answered, "Thinking of something which is absolutely unthinkable (*fu-shiriyo*, not-to-be-thought-of)."*
>
> *The monk asked, "How can one think of anything which is absolutely unthinkable?"*

> *The master said, "By the a-thinking thinking (thinking-which-is-non-thinking)."*

'Non-thinking' does not mean blanking the mind of all thoughts and emotions. People often get caught up in the idea that in meditation you need to 'stop your thoughts' or 'make the mind go blank'. This is utterly self-defeating.

'Non-thinking' means not grasping at anything, no attachment to analysing, judging, dividing, separating.

You do not try *not* to think; if you do so, it is another attachment and it becomes another striving and struggle. Do not try to repress or suppress your thoughts. Merely take note of them and gently come back to your breath-awareness.

There is a Zen story that illustrates the point of bare attention—not-thinking and no not-thinking. Once a woodcutter went to the mountains and saw a strange animal by the tree he was supposed to cut. Frightened, he immediately thought, "I must kill this animal." The animal then spoke to the woodcutter and said, "Are you going to kill me?" Having his mind read, the woodcutter got angry and thought, "I wonder what I should do?" Immediately, the animal said, "Now you are wondering what you should do with me." The animal seemed to be able to read the woodcutter's mind and would reflect every thought of his. Finally, the woodcutter said to himself, "I will stop thinking of what to do with the animal and go on cutting wood." While he was busy cutting wood, the blade of his axe fell off and killed the animal.

You are like the woodcutter, struggling with your thoughts. The more you try to get rid of them the more they come back to you. Like the woodcutter, learn to stop bothering about them. Turn your attention instead to your in-breath and your out-breath, coming back to them over and over again. Eventually, the energy of your awareness will still your tendency to grasp your thoughts and they will no more bother you.

It's the same with emotions. Let them come, let them go. When a strong emotion arises, watch how your body and breath respond. Is your breathing pattern changing, are your muscles contracting? Our emotions are not some phantom figures floating around in the psyche. They are as 'real' as the muscle that bunches and tenses, the breath that heaves and pants, the heart that pounds and pulses; as real as the rush of blood, the sweat in the palms. Be aware of all these sensations. Stay in the awareness for a while. Then gently come back to the breath.

Labelling is an excellent way of dealing with sensations, thoughts and emotions during *zazen*. When you find yourself replaying an incident that made you angry, for instance, don't play out the fantasy scene in your mind. Merely note, 'anger'. Another random thought arises. Note, 'thinking'. You hear a dog barking—tell yourself, 'hearing'. Label each sensation. Pain shoots up your leg. Note, 'feeling'. Of course, the pain persists and the mind is still with it. Note, 'more feeling'.

Remember, in *zazen* there is no attachment, no judging, no criticism. You may get caught up in sensations, thoughts, emotions, fantasies again and again and yet again. It is all right. Come back to the breath, again and again and yet again.

In one mode, you *are* your thoughts; you *are* your emotions, images, ideas, attitudes, judgements, desires, decisions. At the same time you are more than your thoughts and emotions. Your consciousness is the vast space embracing within it all the universe.

Your thoughts are basically the questions that life puts to you as well as the questions you put to life. Sitting in *zazen* is rightly ordering yourself in the space of these questions. Sit with all the questions of your life. Let them be ordered in the light of the beyond-of-thoughts.

This is the way of *zazen*. Not a technique to be learned and mastered. But a way of being and letting be, surrendering and accepting, saying 'yes' to life and reality.

> *Before a step is taken, the goal is reached;*
> *Before the tongue is moved, the speech is finished.*
> *Though you may take the initiative, point by point,*
> *You must know there is the all-surpassing hole.*
>
> — Mumon

Shikantaza:
The *Zazen* of Intimacy

A monk asked Kyorin, "What is the meaning of Bodhidharma coming from the West?"
Kyorin said, "Sitting long and getting tired."

The practice of *zazen*-only (as opposed to the *koan* method) or 'just sitting' is the practice of being present, in the here and the now. The Japanese term for this is *shikantaza*, just sitting, which means non-dual awareness.

Zazen, as I said, is the practice of seeing into your True Self. This is not to say that you try to get from some one point to some other point in *zazen*. It is not a process of going from here to there but a state of letting be, letting go. In *zazen*, you already are there.

Never left home, but always on the way; on the way, but ever at home.

When we sit we are not trying to *achieve* some particular state of consciousness. Not trying to achieve anything, and not trying *not* to achieve anything. No goals, no comparisons, no judgements, no achievements. Just being-there, being present and grounded in awareness. It is, as Dogen says, the 'total exertion' of being oneself and being with oneself.

In a deep sense, *zazen* is consciousness becoming conscious of itself, awareness resting on awareness. It is the transformation of body-mind-universe into a non-dual awareness, where the distinction between subject and object dissolves into oneness that is Emptiness.

We can be in two modes of consciousness and perceiving, or two ways of being. One is that of survival and security, of being somebody as against others: it involves separation, division, analysis, comparison, competition, judgement and struggle. The root of it is imitative or mimetic desire and fear. This we call the ego-self mode and it is bound with anxiety.

The other mode we call the Self mode. It is one of being, unity and openness. This is Self as Emptiness, as openness, as no thing, no object. This Self is beyond dualities, divisions and separations. Here there is no subject and no object, no this against that. There is no fear in it, no anxiety. There is nothing to lose: for the Self is Emptiness. It is also Fullness. There is in it joy, peace, equanimity, love, compassion. No attachments, no obsessions, no demands, no running away. Letting-be oneself just as one is, with all of one's fears, imperfections and vulnerabilities. Accepting to be in mystery, darkness, unknowing. *Zazen* is to let yourself enter this Self-mode of being and consciousness. Realize you are Emptiness, openness, oneness. That is what your mind and heart are. Just *be* that. Not so much in total clarity and purity, but in darkness and unknowing, from where arise transcendental faith and trust and love. You do this by being in touch with your body and breath, in a body-mind-heart act.

This is the practice of *shikantaza:* just sitting, just observing, just being here and now, with no seeking and no goals. It is intimacy with oneself and with the world. This is the *zazen* of intimacy. When you let-be and be with your body sensations and emotions without letting yourself be carried away by fantasy, without acting-out and without repression, there will arise great energy and power as well as freedom.

"Sit like Mount Fuji!" Japanese Zen masters were fond of saying. Clouds swirl around the peak of Mount Fuji, the winds whip it incessantly but it sits majestically, unmoving, eternal. So also, sit unmoving, in quiet majesty and in great dignity, as storm clouds of thoughts, emotions, passions, fantasies rage through your consciousness; let them pass on.

The *zazen* practice of self-forgetting and abiding focused on breath and body is healing and revitalizing. We have a wealth of research data available today that shows that any repetitive activity like breath-following with passive attitude to thoughts is relaxing and healing. When it is joined with the deep faith and trust that flow from this state of silence and stillness, it is deeply healing and 'wholing'. In the Zen way of just sitting, we go a step further. We enter the ground of our self, into the Self mode. This is not merely a matter of belief or faith or trust, but a *knowing* by *experience* what we truly are.

In China, one of the great masters of just sitting was the 12th century Master Hung-chih Cheng-chueh. This is how he described it: "Your body sits silently; your mind is quiescent, unmoving. This is genuine effort in practice... In this silent sitting, whatever realms may appear the mind remains very clear in all details, with everything in its original place."

Everything in its original place means that things are just as they are without your interpretations and grasping. To sit in *shikantaza* is to let things be just as they are. You do not react to the one thousand things that assail your mind—sound, smell, taste, memory, fantasy, emotions, images, ideas—you do not interpret them, you do not engage yourself with them, you do not try to stop them. You simply let them be.

The man who perfected the form and method of *zazen* was the incomparable Master Dogen Kigen, who lived in the 13th century in Japan. To Dogen, posture and practice, sitting and Enlightenment are not two. "Essence and form are not two," declared Dogen. That is, body and mind, Enlightenment and practice, are not two, they are inseparable. Therefore, when you assume the posture of the Buddha, you are no other than the Buddha.

And that is why we say that in the *zazen* of *shikantaza* we *experience* and *express* our Buddhahood. This is in fact the whole premise of the Soto school that Dogen founded. Practice *is* Enlightenment and Enlightenment *is* practice. When we assume the posture of the Buddha in *zazen*, we already *are* the Buddha. So we sit in *zazen*, not to *attain* Buddhahood but to *express* our Buddhahood.

Said Dogen, on the unity of Enlightenment and practice: "The view that practice and Enlightenment are not one is heretical. In the Buddha-dharma they are one. Inasmuch as practice is based on Enlightenment, the practice of a beginner is entirely that of original Enlightenment. Therefore, in giving the instruction for practice, a Zen teacher advises his/her disciples not to seek Enlightenment beyond practice, for practice itself is original Enlightenment. Because it is already Enlightenment of practice, there is no end to Enlightenment; because it is already practice of Enlightenment, there is no beginning to practice."

Sitting on our cushions in *zazen* we already are the Buddha! With each breath, we are realizing our Buddha-nature; with each breath we are expressing our Buddha-nature. Always attentive, always alert, treat every moment and every breath in *zazen* as a precious jewel, to be watched over and guarded.

The way of *shikantaza* is also known as the way of 'silent illumination'. Hold your mind taut as a bowstring, in a constant state of bare-awareness and let yourself enter into the equanimity of non-attachment. As your *zazen* deepens, your awareness opens to infinity and you come to abide in Self as Self. Says Dogen, "Body and mind will of themselves drop away, and your Original Face will manifest."

Writes Master Keizan: "*Zazen* allows a person to clarify the mind-ground and to dwell comfortably in one's Original-nature… *zazen* is entering directly into the ocean-of-Buddha-nature and manifesting the body of the Buddha. The inherent pure and clear mind is actualized in the present moment; the Original-light completely illuminates everywhere."

Dwelling in this undifferentiated oneness and openness, unknowing and mystery, the simple practice of body-breath awareness is healing and liberating. From this ground of your self that is Emptiness, you step into daily life and activities in equanimity, compassion and alertness.

The practice of *zazen* is to die and lose ourselves: to die to and lose our identification with a particular world of meaning and reality. And thence to rise to and as Emptiness, which is Mystery that is graciousness.

An old pond
A frog jumps in—
Plop!

— Basho

The *Zazen* of Equanimity, Joy and Compassion

A monk asked Hyakujo, "What is the most wonderful thing?"
Jo said, "I sit alone on this Great Sublime Peak."
The monk made a bow. Jo struck him.

We talk about disengagement, disinterestedness, bare awareness not only as the practice of *zazen* but also as an attitude that should inform our everyday lives and activities. Is the Zen way devoid of all feeling and emotion, empty of joy and love?

This is a very wrong view of Zen. Because at the heart of Zen is *karuna* (compassion), *upeksha* (equanimity), *mudita* (joy) and *maitri* (loving-kindness).

The equanimity that comes from non-attachment, the *upeksha* that Buddhism teaches, is not mere non-attachment. It does not mean that you do not engage yourself with life, people, events. Rather, the non-attachment of *upeksha* is freedom from attachment to our ideas and ideologies, to our self-images and self-definitions, to our cravings and hatreds; it is liberation from our egoism and narcissism.

It is being open to the world and to others: it is letting the other be the other, affirming, 'It is good that you are'. It is loving-attention to the concrete individual being. It is, to use a Zen term, 'intimacy' with oneself, with others and with the world.

There is a *sutra*, *The Greater Discourse of Advice to Rahula*, which is Buddha's advice to his son on meditation. I like this very much, it is short and beautiful and it exhorts you to cultivate equanimity of mind. It explains clearly all the necessary elements of Theravada meditation, which are of course part of Mahayana and Zen meditation, too.

The first part suggests that you are not your body nor are you material form or emotions and thoughts; you are not to identify with any material or perishable form. 'This is not mine, this I am not, this is not my self.' (This is perhaps what the Buddha originally meant by no-self, *anatma*.)

The second part, which seems to be central to the *sutra*, articulates meditation as equanimity, drawing a comparison with the four great cosmic elements of earth, water, fire and space.

> *Rahula, develop meditation that is like the earth; for when you develop meditation that is like the earth, arisen agreeable and disagreeable contacts will not invade your mind and remain. Just as people throw clean things and dirty things, excrement, urine, spittle, pus, and blood on the earth, and the earth is not horrified, humiliated, and disgusted because of that, so too, Rahula, develop meditation that is like the earth; for when you develop meditation that is like the earth, arisen agreeable and disagreeable contacts will not invade your mind and remain.*

Be like the earth in equanimity, in patience and acceptance. The earth lets-be everything that people do to it, "*clean things and dirty things, excrement, urine, spittle, pus, and blood*". The earth patiently accepts and lets-be all that. So also, in *zazen*, be and let-be, let-be all your so-called negative emotions: fear, anger, darkness, lust and so on.

We tend to get attached to the so-called heavenly emotions and thoughts and we try to avoid all that smacks of hell and darkness. We are preoccupied with identifying ourselves with a particular mode of being and doing, with some one 'name and form'. We are achievers; we want to achieve good meditation, we want to attain to good emotions and thoughts, we want to feel good.

Zazen is to stop trying to run away from ourselves. Just be, let-be. Let-be all of yourself and accept your negative, darker side. Whatever comes into your awareness, take note of it, let it be and go on with your *zazen*. If you try to run away from such thoughts you will be lost; if you try *not* to run away from them you will still be lost.

Zazen is a great Amen. It is saying a great 'Yes' to your existence and being and to all that *is*. It is the great 'Yes' with which the Buddha finally conquered the temptations of Mara.

In the legends, Mara tries to seduce the Buddha by many means but fails in them all. In a last, desperate measure he pulls out the grand temptation: Mara tells the Buddha that the earth on which the Buddha is seated belongs to Mara and orders him to get out of there!

Do you see what this temptation of Mara means? The temptation is to deny one's very self, to disown one's existence and being, to be untrue to one's own vocation; to deny one's body and sexuality, strength and beauty, desires, needs and passions. The temptation orders you: be not yourself, be what I tell you to be.

This is the temptation, our very own Mara, that we face when we sit in *zazen*. This is the temptation that we overcome simply by being there, being present, accepting ourselves, letting be. Rabbi Zusya said, "In the coming world, they will not ask me, 'Why were you not Moses?' They will ask me, 'Why were you not Zusya?'"

The *sutra* repeats the same idea with reference to the elements of fire and water. On space, it adds:

> *Just as space is not established anywhere, so too, Rahula, develop meditation that is like space.*

Your Self is like vast space, bound by nothing, identified with nothing. You are space, in which clouds float by, birds fly, mountains rise up, rain comes down, thunder and lightning flash forth. You are that, you embrace all the universe. You are an openness to all that *is* and happens. Your Self is openness itself. Standing nowhere and yet coming forth here and now. You are the universe, the universe is yourself.

Zazen is the earth sitting, mountains and rivers practising. It is the practice of the whole universe. When you breathe, it is the universe that is breathing. When you walk, it is the universe that is walking. Sit and walk *thus*. Tathagata is one who *thus* comes, or *thus* goes.

The next part of the *sutra* talks of meditation as the practice of developing the four *Brahma Viharas*: loving-kindness (*maitri*), compassion (*karuna*), appreciative or altruistic joy (*mudita*) and equanimity (*upeksha*).

Brahma Viharas can be translated as Divine Abodes; they are also known as Boundless States or the Immeasurables. These are bodhisattva virtues for the liberation of all beings. These are, as is obvious, directed towards others and towards all beings. But you have to arouse them in yourself first, for the sake of others. The Buddha said:

> *Rahula, develop meditation on loving-kindness; for when you develop meditation on loving-kindness, any ill-will will be abandoned.*
>
> *Rahula, develop meditation on compassion; for when you develop meditation on compassion, any cruelty will be abandoned.*

Rahula, develop meditation on appreciative joy; for when you develop meditation on appreciative joy, any discontent will be abandoned.

Rahula, develop meditation on equanimity; for when you develop meditation on equanimity, any aversion will be abandoned.

Zazen is letting the *Brahma Viharas* well up in your heart and mind. It is letting your heart-mind of faith, courage, compassion, joy and equanimity come forth and irradiate your self and the world. These *Brahma Viharas* are unconditional virtues (*paramitas*): they are not the product of your work or merit, nor are they simply caused by others. Other people and circumstances are the occasions and conditions that evoke them.

Our practice is to learn to abide in them in the midst of darkness and suffering, rejection and loss. In *zazen*, we are in touch with all of our negative feelings and emotions, and *at the same time* we are in peace, joy and compassion. We do not try to repress or deny our fears, anxieties, jealousies, angers and the seeming meaninglessness, arbitrary blindness and insignificance of our lives. In the midst of all that and embracing all that, we abide in *bodhicitta*; we abide in it in faith, courage, peace and compassion.

The next part of the *sutra* briefly mentions meditating on the foulness of the body and on impermanence. This is a traditional practice.

The last part of the *sutra* talks about the practice of mindfulness. This part in a sense summarizes and embraces all that has gone before. Mindfulness practice is the central practice of Theravada Buddhism; it is central to all of our practice. (There is a separate *sutra* about mindfulness practice, *Satipatthana Sutra*.) Our brief *sutra* ends with praise of mindfulness: "When mindfulness of breathing is developed and cultivated in this way, even the final in-breath and out-breath are known as they cease, not unknown."

Koan Zen:
The Questing Heart-Mind

Let me tell you a Zen story.
> *Once a monk asked Master Joshu, "What is the meaning of the First Patriarch coming to China?"*
> *Joshu replied, "The cypress tree in front of the courtyard."*
> *The monk was Enlightened.*

Maybe it's not a story, it is a dialogue. You will find many such puzzling dialogues in Zen. All of them involve an apparently nonsensical exchange between two people, usually seeker and master, at the end of which the questioner invariably 'suddenly attained Enlightenment'.

Here is another such encounter:
> *A monk asked Tung-shan, "Who is the Buddha?"*
> *Tung-shan replied, "Three pounds of flax."*
> *The monk was Enlightened.*

Puzzling as they are, these encounters are the very heart of Zen. In the Zen tradition they are called *koans* (from the Chinese *kung-an*). Much has been written and debated about the *koan* system and *satori* (or *kensho*) or 'sudden Enlightenment' with which it is inextricably linked. *Koan* Zen, or 'encounter dialogue', became prominent in China with the Hung-chou school of Ma-tsu who lived in the eighth century, but it is Ta-hui, in the 12th century, who seems to have given form to the modern *koan* practice. It revitalized Zen in China. In fact, many scholars believe that Zen would have died out but for the rigorous *koan* system introduced by these great masters. In the annals of Zen history there are hundreds of recorded instances of *satori*—glimpses of sudden Enlightenment—attained by monks and lay students through *koan* meditation. They are stories that inspire us, show us that every one of us is capable of being Enlightened in this lifetime.

For those of you who are beginners, let me say a few words on *koans*.

I have here a quote from the Zen scholar D T Suzuki that puts it succinctly: "A *koan*, according to one authority, means 'a public document setting up a standard of judgement', whereby one's Zen understanding is tested as to its correctness. A *koan* is generally some statement made by an old Zen master, or some answer of his given to a questioner."

There are a couple of key ideas here that may help you. First is the assertion that *koan* study leads a student to 'Zen understanding' and second, that this understanding is 'tested for its correctness'. 'Zen understanding' here implies not only *satori* or Awakening, but also the deepening of the Awakening in continued *koan* study. *Satori* is not the end of *koan* study, it is the beginning. Secondly, this understanding has to be 'tested as to its correctness': this refers to the master-disciple relationship that is central in *koan* Zen. I will come back to this later.

Traditionally, the three prerequisites of Zen have been said to be: Great Faith, Great Doubt, and Great Questioning, or Seeking and Struggle.

Great Faith is Patriarchal Faith, the faith that affirms: "I *am* Buddha." It is a deep faith and trust in one's Self. This is opposed to Doctrinal Faith, which places belief in an idealized object outside of the self and then affirms: "I can *become* Buddha." Patriarchal Faith arises from reverence for and trust in one's teacher and the words of the Buddha. But our honesty leads us to doubt: "I am an ignorant sentient being. How can I then be the truly Enlightened Buddha?"

The tension and dialectic between these two poles of faith and doubt, affirmation and negation are brought to sharp focus by meditating on the *koan*. *Koan* practice can bring one to a breakthrough, which in Korean Zen tradition is called *kkaech'im*, brokenness. What is broken through is one's dualistic intellectual framework and attachment to ego.

The *koan* in a sense concretizes the ultimate questions that are the heart-mind's quest: what is the meaning of my life? Where do I go after death? What is really Real? Who am I? Hui'ke, the Second Patriarch of Zen, struggles with a heart that is restless and seeks peace. Sosan, the Third Patriarch, yearns to be freed from his sins. Doshin, the Fourth Patriarch, seeks liberation.

There are questions of the intellect: to know and be known; there are questions of the heart: to love and be loved. You cannot ignore the questions of the heart-mind. (The Sino-Japanese word, *hsin/shin*, denotes both heart and mind and so here I use the combination of heart-mind.) In *koan* practice we listen to the deeper questions of the heart-mind and learn to articulate them. The *koan* stands in the place of all your life questions. It gives a 'handle' to the search and the struggle.

> *Think neither good nor evil. At that very moment, what is your Primal Face?*

This is the famous *koan* that the Sixth Patriarch gave Myo, the deluded, greedy monk. It is a question that continues to be asked of students in Zen centres even today. It is a question for you. Tell me, who are you truly?

Your Original Face before your parents were born. That is, your Self beyond all dualities such as good and bad, body and mind, time and eternity, and so on. Who are you truly? Are you only your history, social status and physical form or are you more than these? Are you only your relationships, loves and friends? Who are you before the world, before others, and to yourself?

> The monk Nangaku Ejo came to visit the Sixth Patriarch Eno and the latter asked him, "What is this that has come thus?" After eight years of struggle and seeking, Nangaku came to Awakening and gave his answer: "Whatever I say I am will miss the point."

That, exactly, is the real 'I'. The Self cannot be captured by concepts or images. It is not one, it is not two. It is not the same, it is not different. The interrogative words such as what, who, why, whence in the 'encounter dialogues' point to the ultimate truth of thusness. They point to and express the inexpressible, the unknowable, the unnamable, the unutterable. They are utterances asserting nothing. The questions dislodge you from your settled positions, ideas, opinions or statements. They challenge you to realize your Formless Self, your Original Face. But the Formless Self is no other than the form of this very self.

Before I go further I would like to come back to a question asked very often of me by my students. Is there any 'technique' to working on *koans*? In *koan* practice, 'become the *koan*'—realize that you *are* the *koan*.

Mumon, the author of one of the first collections of *koans* in China, called *Mumonkan*, describes how to work on the *koan* '*Mu*'. The *koan* goes:

A monk asked Joshu, "Does a dog have Buddha-nature or not?" Joshu said, "Mu." (Mu in Chinese means 'no'.)

Here is what Mumon advises: "… make your whole body a mass of doubt, and with your 360 bones and joints, your 84,000 hair follicles, concentrate on the one word 'Mu'. Day and night, keep digging into it. Don't consider it to be meaningless. Don't think in terms of 'has' or 'has not'. It is like swallowing a red-hot iron ball. You try to vomit it out, but you cannot… Suddenly, Mu breaks open… Exhaust all your life-energy on this one word Mu. If you do not falter, then it's done! A single spark lights your Dharma candle."

In most Zen schools, the first basic *koan* is Joshu's *Mu koan*. *Mu* leads one to a complete letting go of oneself and to deep insight. However, one can enter through any 'gate' and the teacher usually decides what is appropriate for the student.

The Zen master occupies a central place in this *koan* journey. The master is there not so much to give assurances or answers: he is primarily there to help evoke, provoke, destroy and restructure your questions. He is there to authenticate your Realization. In the Zen tradition, as in most mystical or spiritual traditions, your Awakening is not valid, recognized, or complete until it has been tested and authenticated by your teacher.

The expression and presentation of your *koan* is the life-breath of your spiritual journey in *koan* Zen. Indeed, the presenting and actualization of yourself in dialogue is itself the Realization and the authentication. This Realization-authentication has to be further tested and attested to in your everyday life. But in the dialogue with the master, it is not so much what is presented as how it is presented that is significant. You learn to 'forget' yourself and you let yourself go, in action, in 'becoming' the *koan*. Can you surrender yourself to your being here and now completely and present yourself in thusness?

Do not literalize the *koan*s and answers. Do not be stuck with the so-called 'correct' answers. At the same time, you must be exact and to the point in your response. Now how will you respond to your *koan*?

A deep Realization will flow freely in the authentication process. But you need also to learn the Zen idiom and language. Korean Zen Master Seung Sahn talks of three kinds of Enlightenment answers. For example, to the question 'What is this?' of an apple, to answer "an apple" can mean that you are caught by a name. To say "not an apple" may mean you are attached to Emptiness or negation. On the other hand, if you hit the floor or shout "*katz*" you throw away all names and no-names, it is presenting Emptiness. (In Zen idiom, the shout '*katz*' means that one has thrown away all ideas and concepts, that one has experienced Emptiness, that one is no more attached to anything.) It is called the 'first Enlightenment'. Next comes 'original Enlightenment', which is to answer, "the sky is blue, the grass is green, the wall is white, the apple is red". It is a 'like this' answer, and means that things are as they are; it is three times three equals nine. The third is 'final Enlightenment': you take the apple and have a bite of it. This is a 'just like this' answer.

All this is helpful, but there is a danger of stereotyped actions and answers. It may reduce Zen and Zen dialogue to tactics, tricks, techniques and gimmicks. Correct answers need not mean authentic Realization. There are levels and stages of Awakening and Enlightenment. And your responses will be, or have to be, in accordance with the level. The answer must be fitting and appropriate.

All of our life is a dialogue and exchange, listening and responding. The encounter with the master is also such a dialogue and exchange, but it is about ultimate reality, of who you truly are ultimately. Such dialogue is still only a window into the life you are called to live in the world. Life is the 'master'.

Let me tell you a Zen story that shows the faith, trust, earnestness and determination of the student and how these are tested, challenged and purified. It shows also some of the different stages of Enlightenment, and how one can be caught or can get stuck in one or the other. The story itself is highly stylized, but instructive nevertheless.

A student once approached Zen Master Hyang Bong and beseeched him to teach him the Dharma. Hyang Bong turned him away, saying his Dharma was too expensive. The student pulled out the few coins in his pocket, which were the sum of his worldly possessions, and offered them to the teacher. Hyang Bong still refused to teach.

The student went away to practise by himself, but was back after a few months. This time, he offered the teacher his life. But all Hyang Bong would say was, "My Dharma is too expensive for that."

Off went the student, to return in a few months offering his mind. Hyang Bong said, "Your mind is a pail of garbage, and even if you offered me ten thousand minds, my Dharma would still be too expensive."

The student threw himself into his practise, and came to the understanding that the universe is "empty". He went to the master and said he understood how expensive his Dharma was. How expensive, asked the master. "*Katz!*" shouted the student. Hyang Bong shook his head and said, "My Dharma is more expensive than that."

This time, the student was determined not to go back without a great Awakening. Finally, it happened, and the student ran excitedly to the master and shouted, "Master, now I truly understand: the sky is blue, the grass is green." But Hyang Bong merely said "My Dharma is even more expensive than that."

This was too much for the student, and he screamed, "I don't need your Dharma, you can take it and shove it up your ass!" With that, he rushed headlong towards the door. Just as he was going out of the door, Hyang Bong called to him, "Wait a minute!" The student turned his head. "Don't lose my Dharma," said Hyang Bong. Upon hearing these words, the student was truly Enlightened.

When you have come to deep, authentic Realization, you will throw away *koans* and *koan* answers and you will walk freely between heaven and earth.

Tell me, what was your Original Face before you were born?

Teisho

Teisho is the formal talk given by the Zen master to students during *sesshin* (intensive periods of Zen practice). Delivered every day of the *sesshin* between periods of *zazen*, it is an integral part of the practice, and is one of the most sacred rituals in the Zen tradition.

While *teisho* is a formal talk, it is not to be equated with a philosophical discourse. No doctrines or formulae are lectured upon. Rather, *teisho* is an expression of the heart-mind of the master, an expression of his own Realization. Sometimes picturesque, often anecdotal and full of allusions, *teisho* is a pointer to the Truth that the student must discover by herself/himself and make it her/his own. Questions, that will immediately make a theory of what has been said, are entirely discouraged, either during or after the *teisho*.

In a tradition where the master-disciple relationship plays a significant role, *teisho* is one of the formal points of contact between the master and student and is therefore sacrosanct. The other point of contact is during *dokusan/sanzen*, or the one-on-one 'interview' where the student 'confronts' the master with the understanding she/he has gained from her/his practice. This is a chance for the student to challenge the master, not through philosophical debate but by expressing or manifesting her/his own understanding and testing it with that of the master. *Dokusan/sanzen* is a strictly private process where all talk not pertaining to practice is taboo.

Zen Master AMA Samy's *teisho* typically centres on a *koan* on which he gives a 'commentary'. This works at different levels. For beginners, it recreates the context and spirit of the *koan*. Advanced students whose minds are primed by the preceding hours of *zazen* may, with right words from the master, suddenly come to a deep, intuitive understanding.

This section contains a collection of *teishos* given by Master AMA Samy, and constitutes the core of his teachings. The structure of all of them is the same: starting with the *koan* on which the Master gives a commentary and ending with a *koan* with which the Master confronts his students. It would be worth pointing out that the commentary is by no means an intellectual analysis of or dissertation on the *koan* in question, though many philosophical pointers are given. Rather, it is an enactment of the heart-mind of the seeker who plumbs its mysterious depths to uncover the Great Truth that it enfolds.

The talks have been edited to suit this publication; for example, quotations have been inserted and references expanded and substantiated. The overall structure has been tightened. Unavoidably, the written text loses some of the verve and vitality of the talks. However, care has been taken to retain, as far as possible, the distinctive style and expression of the Master. Repetitions, for reiteration, are integral to the style of teaching and have therefore been left unedited.

Editor

Part I

Your Original Face

Your Original Face Before You Were Born

Hui-neng, who had been named Sixth Patriarch but was fleeing his monastery on the advice of his master, was pursued by the monk Myo as far as Mount Daiyu. Suddenly, Hui-neng put down the robe and bowl that were the symbols of transmission and said, "This robe represents the faith. How can it be competed for by force? I will allow you to take it away."

Myo tried to lift it up, but it was as immovable as a mountain. Terrified and trembling with awe, he said, "I came for the Dharma, not the robe. I beg you, please reveal it to me."

Hui-neng said, "Think neither good nor evil. At that very moment, what is the primal face of Monk Myo?"

In that instant, Myo suddenly attained deep Realization. In tears, he bowed and said, "Besides the secret words and secret meaning you have just now revealed to me, is there anything else deeper yet?"

Hui-neng said, "What I have now preached to you is no secret at all. If you reflect on your own true face, the secret will be found in yourself."

> Myo said, "Though I have been at Obai with the other monks, I never realized what my True Self is. Now, thanks to your instruction, I know it is like a man who drinks water and knows for himself whether it is cold or warm. Now you, lay brother, are my master." Hui-neng said, "If that is the way you feel, let us both have Obai for our master. Be mindful and hold fast to what you have realized."

Hui-neng was the Sixth Patriarch of Zen. He was a poor, illiterate woodcutter. One day, while selling wood, he heard someone reading from the Diamond Sutra and was deeply moved by the phrase, "Dwelling nowhere, the mind comes forth." This set him in search of a master who could help him come to true Awakening, and thus he came to the Fifth Patriarch. The Fifth Patriarch asked him, "Where do you come from?"

"From Reinan (south of the mountain), Master."

"What are you seeking?"

"To become Buddha."

"You barbarians of Reinan do not have Buddha-nature. How can you expect to become a Buddha?"

Hui-neng replied, "Though there is south and north for man, how can there be a south and north for Buddha-nature?"

This showed the spiritual depth of Hui-neng. But he was a layman and newcomer, so in order not to provoke trouble from the monks, he was sent to help in the kitchen.

Soon, it was time for the Fifth Patriarch to find his successor. He asked his monks to compose a verse manifesting each one's Enlightened heart-mind. The leader of the monks composed his verse, but he was afraid of taking it to the master; so he put it up on the monastery wall—if it was good, he would be called, if not, nobody would bother:

> *The body is the Bodhi tree,*
> *The mind is a clear mirror stand.*
> *Wipe it clean moment by moment*
> *Never let dust and rubbish adhere to it.*

This verse portrays the 'gradual approach' to Enlightenment in Zen: work hard, struggle with yourself and the world, be ever awake and vigilant, hold on to what you have. It focuses on human effort and reflects a somewhat dualistic vision of reality. Mind is, so to say, the mirror of nature: keep it pure and spotless, so that the true nature can be mirrored in its purity. Our illiterate assistant cook heard of it. On an impulse he asked someone to write his verse beside the first one:

> *The Bodhi is intrinsically no tree;*
> *Nor has the clear mirror any stand.*
> *There is not one thing from the beginning,*
> *Where can dust and rubbish adhere at all?*

The legend goes that seeing this verse, the Fifth Patriarch went to the kitchen, called for Hui-neng, gave him thirty blows and named him his successor and Sixth Patriarch of Zen. I must mention at this point that scholars have questioned the historicity of this story. The verse/counter verse competition probably never took place, and the verses in fact seemed to have been composed decades apart. But the second verse is undoubtedly that of Hui-neng and reflects his True Awakening.

"There is not one thing from the beginning." There is neither mind nor nature! This is the hallmark of Zen, of the 'sudden' approach. It is the diamond sword that cuts through the thousand and one knots of the human heart and mind. When Bodhidharma was asked by Emperor of Liang, "What is the first principle of the holy teachings?" he replied, "Emptiness, no holiness." This is your True Self, your Self before your mother and father were born. It is not an objective world, nor is it the subjective world. It is your heart-mind, it is the heart-mind of heaven and earth.

Coming back to the story: after he named Hui-neng his successor and gave him his robe and bowl as a symbol of the transmission, the Fifth Patriarch knew that the monks were not going to take this transmission to a lay newcomer lying down. Zen monks are not immune to greed, envy, rivalry, hatred and stories about this are legion. So he advised Hui-neng to go away immediately and practise secretly for some years before he came forth into the world to teach and lead. The *koan* begins here.

When the monks learnt what had happened, they were furious and went in pursuit of the dharma 'thief'. It was a long and arduous hunt. What are they searching for? They had come in search of the true Dharma, in quest of Awakening. But what are they now running after? Almost all of the pursuing monks dropped out on the way from sheer exhaustion, except a strong and determined one, a monk called Myo, who was an ex-general. Myo caught up with Hui-neng on Mount Daiyu.

Hui-neng laid down the robe and the bowl, and told Myo, "Please take it; this is only a symbol of faith and trust. Is that what you came for?" Myo was stunned: is that what he had come for, to become a monk and labour all his life? In Jesus' parable of the Prodigal Son, the prodigal son, in the depth of his misery is said to have 'come to himself' and thus begun his journey back home. Myo now comes to himself and with tears begs, "I came for the Dharma, not for the robe, please help me." Hui-neng functions as the true master and calls Myo to his True Self: "Think neither of good nor of evil. At this very moment, what is your Original Face, your Original Face before your mother and father were born?" What is your ultimate reality? Who are you truly? Who Am I?

The scales fell from the eyes of Myo and he suddenly Awakened. The self Awakens to the Self. His Self before he was born—before his mother and father were born. "Think neither good nor evil": the reference here is not to ethics or morality. It is to the realm of the Self that is beyond all dualities and relativities. Our ordinary selfhood and self-image are defined in terms of dualities: of past, present and future; in terms of people, places, experiences; in terms of good and bad, problems and antinomies, limits and boundaries, life and death, heaven and hell. We find ourselves bound by birth and death, by karma and rebirth, by our thoughts and emotions, the demands and expectations of others and ourselves, and so on. This is the world of *samsara* and we find our usual identity in *samsara*. It is the world of desire and of *dukkha*. Can you Awaken in the midst of this world, in the midst of your *samsaric* life, here and now and not *after* solving all your life-problems and conflicts?

Standing in the midst of all his suffering, greed and illusions, Myo Awakens to the Self that is Emptiness: *from the beginning there is no thing at all!* No thing to grasp, no thing to flee from, nothing that limits and defiles his Self. It is Emptiness Awakening to Emptiness! *That* is his Self, the Formless Self. Standing nowhere, the mind comes forth. The bird sings, the river flows; the sky is blue, the rose is red.

With tears flowing from his heart and mind, Myo asks the Sixth Patriarch, "Are there any more secrets and hidden depths?" Why, it is no secret at all! It is your very Self manifesting here and now. See how red that flower is and how green that leaf is. The whole world is transparent, manifesting in suchness.

> *A monk once asked Master Kyorin, "What is the meaning of Bodhidharma coming from the West?"*

(That is to say, what is the ultimate secret meaning

or ultimate reality?) Kyorin answered, "Sitting long and getting tired."

A monk asked the same question to Master Joshu, "What is the meaning of Bodhidharma coming from the West?" Joshu replied, "The oak tree in the front garden."

When Myo comes to Realization, he says in astonishment, "Now I know, it is like a man who drinks water and knows for himself whether it is cold or warm." Realizing Emptiness is not an abstraction, not a theory, not an opinion. It is the Self Awakening to the Self. It is your heart-mind coming home to the peace of heart and mind. If there is no such peace of heart-mind, if there is no such Realization, it will, in Zen language, be 'the distance between heaven and hell'.

Mumon in his beautiful verse to this *koan* exclaims, "It can't be described! It can't be pictured! It can't be sufficiently praised! Stop trying to do something with it!" Yet he goes on to proclaim, "There is nowhere to hide the primal face."

Let me tell you another Zen story. There was once a monk who had attended on his master for many years. He was unhappy that even after all that time he had not realized the secret of Zen. So one day he complained to the master about his ignorance. The master took him into the garden. He asked the monk if he heard the bird sing. Yes, he did. Did he see the flowers and their beauty? Yes, he did. The master said, "See, I have not hidden anything from you!"

A similar story runs like this: after many years of serving the master, a monk asked him when he would begin teaching him Zen. The master replied, "When you brought me tea, did I not receive it? When I called you, did you not respond? How can you then say that I have not been teaching you the truth? From morning till evening, there has been teaching and you have been responding admirably!"

Ultimate reality is not apart from this calling and the responding. Every thing, every moment, is calling you and asking you for a response. How do you respond? Where do you come from? Who calls and who answers?

Sometimes, there can be deep, transforming experiences. However, one cannot experience or see Emptiness itself; for the self is not apart from Emptiness. As the eye cannot see itself, so the Self cannot see itself reflexively. However, it can be intuited and realized. Or rather, the Self Awakens to the Self, consciousness becomes conscious of itself. But this Realization comes about in letting-go oneself and in letting-be the other. In opening oneself to the other/world, in letting be the other, Emptiness is realized, Self is actualized. Realizing Emptiness is not apart from realizing that the Self is the world, the world is the Self. Not in a static way, but in the act of self-emptying; it is the process of emptying Emptiness itself!

The world and you are not two; when you are in an openness-state, the world and reality 'enter' you; at those times, the flower is yourself, the bird is yourself, the crying child is yourself. Huang-po said, "It is self-nature and self-nature alone, absolutely empty and open to all things."

G May describes such experiences as unitive experiences. These unitive experiences, he says, are quite common, for we are basically and fundamentally one with all of reality. It is only that we do not take note of it. But sometimes, in the midst of our whirlwind lives, there come to us deep and unique experiences. You see a flower; there is nothing but the flower in the whole universe. You hear a piece of music; there is nothing but that music in the entire universe. You have become at that moment the flower, the music. Such unitive experience is first of all an experience, of being–at–one. All self-defining activities cease; there is in those moments, no self-definition, no self-image, no thought of 'I am at–one', or of me, mine and I as opposed to others; no idea of oneself controlling, accomplishing, or even of doing anything; no intent, no memory, no aspiration and no conscious fear. Time seems to stop. However, body sense is preserved; you can say 'me' in unitive experience without being self-defining. 'The sky is blue, the grass is green.'

Secondly, unitive experience is change in awareness; all focusing attention ceases, awareness is opened up. "All the senses are acute, but there is no mental labelling or reaction concerning sensory stimuli. The water is very clear and calm… While there may be a difference in degree of opening of awareness, the fact that awareness opens is a constant criterion for unitive experience. Any preoccupation or restriction of attention is self-defining and thus precludes a full unitive experience."

Let's examine this by example. When the monk Myo runs after Hui-neng in pursuit of the robe and bowl, is he in the state of unitive experience? Myo's attention is focused solely on the robe and bowl, there is no other image or thought in him, he is single-minded. But you can see that his is one-track awareness, he is carried away by desire and greed, his awareness is not a disinterested and open one, but closed and blinded by greed and envy. He is not in self-losing mode, but self-seeking one.

The third factor of unitive experience is the reaction to the experience at the end of it or afterwards. This third phase is the reflective phase; this is where we talk about our experience, know that *we* have had it. This is also the point where illusions and dualisms enter. There may be warmth and love, but also some fear and anxiety, for the ego has been dethroned and threatened.

We are tempted to hold on to or seek out a repeat of such experiences. Very often, though, we just ignore these moments and carry on with our lives in forgetfulness.

The unitive experience is an altered state of consciousness. Consciousness is state-specific. That is to say, it is correlative to the state and condition you are in. For example, think of the times you have been deeply angry, or loving, or concerned and so on. In each of these states, your awareness and consciousness were different, in accordance with the state. Knowledge, too, is dependent on the state of our consciousness. Dream states, drug-induced states, love states, ordinary states: normally you will not be able to access the knowledge you have in one state while you are in another. The knowledge and consciousness of the non-dual state cannot be accessed by and in the dualistic state; but the dualistic state and its conditions can usually be accessed in the non-dual state.

Each state of consciousness is correlative of a particular self or sub-self. You have many kinds of consciousness and many selves. But there is no value in being attached to any of these states of consciousness! Even if these states are the blissful states of love or passion, it is of no use to be attached to them. For there is more to us than that state. So to be attached to one state of consciousness or one sub-self would be to diminish ourselves.

In very much the same way, to be attached to the experience of the non-dual consciousness is but illusion and egoism. You already are one and non-dual with all of reality. Just look at the flower, just hear that bird singing; at the moment of hearing and seeing, the song is your self, the flower is your self. Even this is relatively easy.

What is most important, and what we are called to do, is to live from the Realization of oneness and non-duality in our ordinary life. In ordinary, daily life, Realization of Emptiness is a matter of living and loving wholeheartedly—seeing, hearing, and responding to life and reality. One is being called, one answers. It is a matter of being addressed and responding accordingly. In being called and responding, one loses oneself and finds oneself. It is in being thus open to the world and the other that you realize your self as Emptiness. It is the Self responding to the Self.

Emptiness is your Self. Once you Awaken to this, you move freely in duality and non-duality, in oneness and manyness, in silence and speech. To *seek* non-duality and oneness is to fall into dualism and attachment. Once you have Awakened to the mystery of Emptiness that is the ground of your self, your Realization has to flow into dialogue with others and the world, in response and action, in give-and-take. Seng-ts'an sings in his beautiful *On Believing in the Mind*:

> *If you wish to move in the One Way,*
> *Do not dislike even the world of senses and ideas.*
> *Indeed, to accept them fully*
> *Is identical with true Enlightenment.*

A *koan* runs like this:

> *Ananda, the faithful monk-attendant of the Buddha,*
> *asked the great sage Mahakashyapa in all earnestness,*
> *"The World Honoured One transmitted the brocade*
> *robe to you. What else did he transmit to you?"*
> *Kashyapa called, "Ananda!"*
> *Ananda replied, "Yes, Master."*
> *Kashyapa said, "Knock down the flagpole at the gate."*

In responding to the call of Kashyapa with his whole heart and mind, Ananda reveals the secret hidden to the world. Knock down the flagpole means, "There, that is it!" or, "There, now you have realized it!"

Mumon gives a fine verse to this episode:
Some say the answer is more familiar than the question.
How many discuss this with glaring eyes!
Elder brother calls, younger brother answers—the family skeleton.
This is the spring that does not belong to yin and yang.

Calling and answering—it is a delicate dance. Standing nowhere, the heart-mind comes forth. Your self is neither here nor there: it stands in the in-between; it comes forth in the response and action. It is one action, one action of the whole universe.

Let me end with a longish but beautiful *mondo*. 'Seamless pagoda' is the central image of the *mondo* or *koan*. It points to the Formless Self, the Self with no form, which is Emptiness itself. How do you present the Formless Self?

In the *koan*, The National Teacher sits in silence, and presents his very self just as the Buddha presented his very self as an answer long ago. The Formless Self is manifesting itself and hiding itself! It is Emptiness bodying forth and disappearing—'self-emptying'—at the same time. It is not a matter of just the individual self as such. It is the Formless Self manifesting itself as the body of the entire universe—'South of Sho and north of Tan', as the disciple Tangen presents in poetic imagery. Each line of Tangen's verse is here interlaced by the compiler Setcho's verse, which adds to the beauty and architecture:

Emperor Shukuso asked Chu Kokushi (the National Teacher), "When you are a hundred years old (when you are dead), *what shall I do for you?"*
"Make a seamless pagoda for this old monk," answered Kokushi.
"What style is it to be?" the emperor asked.

> *Kokushi was silent for a while, and then he asked,
> "Do you understand?"*
> *"No, I do not," said the emperor.*
> *"I have a disciple called Tangen," said Kokushi,
> "who has the Dharma Seal transmitted by me. He
> is well versed in this matter. Ask him, please."*
> *After Kokushi's death, the emperor summoned
> Tangen and asked him about it. Tangen said,
> "South of Sho and north of Tan,*
> *[Setcho says, "Soundless sound of one hand."]*
> *In between, gold abounds.*
> *[Setcho says, "A staff of a mountain kind."]*
> *The ferryboat under the shadowless tree,*
> *[Sectho says, "Clear is the river, calm is the sea."]*
> *No holy one in the emerald palace you see."*
> *[Setcho says, "All is finished."]*

Setcho's verse:
> *A seamless pagoda, it is difficult to describe;
> The dragon does not thrive in a placid lake.
> Tier after tier, superbly it casts its shadow;
> Let it be admired for a thousand ages.*

Snow Heaped
in a Silver Bowl

The Buddha once narrated a parable in a *sutra*: A man travelling across a field encountered a tiger. He fled, the tiger after him. Coming to a precipice, he caught hold of the root of a wild vine and swung himself down over the edge. The tiger sniffed at him from above. Trembling, the man looked down and found, far below, another tiger waiting to pounce on him. Only the vine sustained him. Suddenly he noticed two mice, one white and one black, gnawing away at the vine little by little. Hanging precariously, the man saw a luscious strawberry near him. Clasping the vine with one hand, he reached out, plucked the strawberry with the other and popped it into his mouth. How sweet it tasted!

This parable is about our human condition. Human life is precarious and fragile. Death, as the tiger in the parable, is facing us above and below, moment by moment. Time in the form of day and night is, like the mice, gnawing at the slender cord holding us to life. But we humans are blind to our situation; we only want to forget ourselves in instant pleasures and enjoyments.

Master Kyogen presented the plight of the human condition to his monks in this famous *koan*:

> *It is like a man up a tree who hangs from a branch*
> *by his mouth; his hands cannot grasp a bough, his*

feet cannot touch the tree. Another man comes under the tree and asks him the meaning of Bodhidharma coming from the West. If he does not answer, he does not meet the questioner's need. If he answers, he will lose his life. At such a time, how should he answer?

Of course, it is you who are asked to respond. When you are facing life and death, how do you respond? Which means, how do you find liberation from impermanence, suffering, mortality and death? Time consumes everything. It is the roaring void, swallowing all beings. In Sanskrit, time is called Kaala, the god of death. All things are changing, all things are impermanent. This is a condition that applies to the whole of the cosmos. But the Buddha's teaching of impermanence is not so much cosmological as a call to us to Awakening and salvation.

There is a story that gives a humorous twist to the *koan*: a man is hanging by a precipice. He prays fervently to god to save him. A voice asks him, "Do you really believe that I can save you? And if yes, are you willing to obey my word?" The man answers, "Yes, Lord, I believe you can save me and I am willing to do whatever you ask of me, absolutely." The voice says, "Good, now let go of your hold on the branch." There is a pause, and then the man looks up and calls, "Is there somebody else up there who can help me?"

In the face of death and impermanence we have devised various ways of coping with our fears and anxieties. All these ways are largely to do with the means of annulling the precariousness and uncertainty of life, to find permanence and surety in some secure ground. Sociologists tell us that primitive man found a sense of permanence and security in the rhythms and forces of the cosmic order. The cosmic forces and cycles of nature became gods of necessity and fate.

But some time in what one scholar has referred to as the axial period, between the 8th and 2nd centuries BCE, the cosmological certainty dissolved and there occurred a revelation of a dimension of reality transcending that of the intra-cosmic gods and forces: in India, in the Upanishadic Brahman/Atman and the Buddha's Nirvana; in Greece, Plato's 'being beyond being' and Aristotle's 'unmoved mover'; in Judaism, the revelation of YHWH, 'I AM THAT I AM' to Moses; in China, the Tao which was beyond name and form. This was a transcendent ground of salvation and security. It was also this transcendent ground from which time and history issued forth. So one now had to take responsibility for the world and history.

But access to that transcendent ground is possible only through faith and activation of inner processes. Such deep, unrelenting faith, coupled with the responsibility for the world and history, seems to be too much for humanity to bear! So, once again we see people seeking security in intra-cosmic gods and some ground in a wild range of beliefs like determinism, 'nature' destiny, matter, the unconscious, laws of history and so on. Of course, people also seek security in building empires, ideologies, sciences, drugs, sex, relationships, work and so on.

There are religious systems that deny change and time; they call the phenomenal world of change and time *maya*, illusion or unreality. For many others, there is only change and time: you just have to accept your impermanence and death, that is all there is to spirituality and religion.

I have been very simplistic in my historical summary. But the point I'm trying to make is that we have constantly sought and found no secure ground anywhere in the world, neither in our individuality nor in our collective commonality or nature or science. Nor does it do any good to hold that change and impermanence are themselves the sure ground. "Impermanence is Buddha-nature," Dogen declared. If Buddha-nature is identified with impermanence as such, how can it be saving reality?

In becoming aware of impermanence we go beyond impermanence; authentic acceptance of impermanence is surrendering to that which transcends impermanence. This is how the Buddha sees deliverance: "That sphere (*ayatana*) exists, monks, where there is no earth, no water, no heat and no wind, where the sphere of infinite space does not exist, nor that of infinite consciousness, nor that of neither-perception-nor-non-perception; there is neither this world nor the other world, neither moon nor sun; there, I say, there is no coming and going, no duration of life, to be followed by death and rebirth; it is not stationed, it is without occurrence(s), and has no object. This, indeed, is the end of suffering."

Again, "There exists, monks, that in which there is no birth, where nothing has come into existence, where nothing has been made, where there is nothing conditioned. If that in which there is no birth... did not exist, no escape here from what is born, become, made conditioned would be known. But since there is that in which there is no birth, where nothing has come into existence, where nothing has been made, where there is nothing conditioned, an escape here for what is born, become, made, conditioned is known."

The Buddha is proclaiming a reality that is called Nirvana as the ultimate liberation and salvation. It is transcendent reality that is at the same time inmost of the inmost; one can come to know it intimately, but one cannot describe it. It is neither merely subjective nor merely objective; neither inside nor outside; neither self nor world nor other world. It is not a cipher, a mere null and void. It is real yet inconceivable. If there were not this reality, there would be no liberation for humans. It does not belong to time and space, but it does not negate time and space; rather it creates and lets be time and world.

Once Kyozan asked his master, Isan, about the hiding place of the true Buddha. In reply, Isan said, "By the ineffable subtlety of thinking without thinking, turn your attention inwards to reflect on the infinite power of the divine spark. When your thinking can go no farther, it returns to its source, where Nature and Form eternally abide, where phenomenon and noumenon are not dual but one. It is there that abides the Suchness of the true Buddha."

Rinzai (Chinese Lin-chi) portrays this reality as not apart from this world and ourselves: "What is this thing called Dharma? Dharma is the Dharma, or Truth, of the mind. The Dharma of the mind has no fixed form; it penetrates all the ten directions. It is in operation right before our eyes. But because people don't have enough faith, they cling to words, cling to phrases. They try to find the Dharma of the Buddhas by looking in written words, but they're as far away from it as heaven is from earth."

This reality is other to you, you are not other to it; it is you, you are not it, as Tozan Ryokai puts it. Master Tozan articulates this 'not-two and not-one' dimension poetically:

Snow heaped up in a silver bowl,
A white heron hidden in the light of the full moon,
The two are alike, yet not the same,
Interfused, yet each having its own place.

The Self is other to you, and yet It is you. It is by being present to the Self as the Self that you realize the Self. It is by abiding in the Self that you can truly 'forget' yourself. Only in coming to know this Self—'merging with thusness'—do you come to deliverance and salvation. But this knowledge is beyond conceptualization and imagination. It is experiential faith, it is intimate knowing.

Let me use another metaphor: your self is both the silent depths of the ocean and the waves on the surface; you most often identify with the waves and are carried away by them. But you are also the depths, though the depth cannot in toto be identified with yourself. The depth has been very beautifully and very enigmatically described as the "self before the eon of Emptiness" in the *Transmission of Light*. A verse in the book related to the metaphor is very evocative:

The ancient stream, the cold spring—no one looks in;
It does not allow travellers to tell how deep it is.

Learn to abide in the depths, unmoved by the waves. The waves are not apart from the silent, mysterious depths of the ocean; still, they are not simply the depths. Of course, this is an inadequate image, and no image can really do justice to the reality. Master Keizan makes this comment on the verse: "Don't look inside, don't seek outside. Don't try to quiet your thoughts or rest your body. Just know intimately, cut off all at once, sit for a while and see. Though you may say there is no place in the four quarters to take a step and no place in the world to fit your body, ultimately you should not depend on the power of another. When you see in this way, there are no skin, flesh, marrow, or bones set out for you. Birth and death, coming and going, cannot change you. Having shed your skin completely, one true reality alone exists. It shines throughout all time, with no distinction of measure or time. Is this only to be called 'before the empty eon'? This place is totally beyond distinctions of before and after."

Master Rinzai uses the image of the True Person of No Rank, and it is more than a mere image:

One day the master took his seat in the lecture hall
and said, "Over the bulky mass of your reddish flesh

(i.e. the physical body) *there is a True Person without any rank. He is constantly coming in and going out through the gates of your face* (i.e. your sense organs). *If you have not yet encountered him, catch him, catch him here and now!"*

At that moment a monk came out and asked, "What kind of a fellow is this True Person?"

The master jumped down from the platform, grabbed the monk, and urged him, "Tell me, tell me!" The monk hesitated. The master at once thrust him away saying, "Ah, what a useless dirt-scraper this True-Person-without-rank of yours is!" And he went away to his room.

This True Person of No Rank, who is that? How do you realize this Person? It is not a matter of simple identity with oneself. It is yourself and it is not. 'Not-two and not-one' is the way one has to understand this. Such a consciousness is in a sense a divided consciousness; it 'stands nowhere'. *Standing nowhere, let the mind come forth*. It is in 'coming forth' in response and action that wholeness and selflessness are realized. You are called and you respond. It is in responding to the call of life and reality that you forget yourself and realize the True Self. The Self is realized in the in-between of call and response, dialogue and action. Yet action alone is not enough, though action and response are the acid test of truth and reality.

Dayang asked Zen master Liangshan, "What is the formless site of Enlightenment?" Liangshan pointed to an icon of the bodhisattva of Compassion and said, "This was painted by Mr. Wu." Dayang was about to say something, when Liangshan grabbed

> him and demanded, "This is the one with form—
> which is the formless one?" At these words Dayang
> attained Enlightenment.

Dayang composed a poem to express his Enlightenment, the last two lines of which are:

> *Release a blackbird by night,*
> *And it flies covered with snow.*

It points to the formless coming inextricably clothed in form.

> *In his last illness, Tokusan was asked, "Is there still*
> *the one who is never sick?"*
> *Tokusan said, "Yes, there is."*
> *"Tell me something about this never-sick one."*
> *Tokusan cried, "Oya, oya!" signalling intense pain.*

Now tell me, where is the Formless One who is never sick?

Coming Home

Whenever he was asked about Zen, Master Gutei simply stuck up one finger. He had a boy attendant to whom a visitor once asked, "What kind of teaching does your master give?" The boy held up one finger, too. Hearing of this, Gutei cut off the boy's finger with a knife. As the boy ran away screaming in pain, Gutei called to him. The boy turned his head and Gutei stuck up one finger. The boy was suddenly Enlightened.

Master Gutei belongs to the 9th century; not much is known of him. The story goes that Gutei was living in a mountain hut. One day a nun by the name of Jissai, meaning 'true world', came to visit him. Without taking off her hat or sandals, which was not very polite of her, she entered the hut, walked thrice around the seat of Gutei, and told him, "If you can say a turning (Zen) word, I will take off my hat and sandals and pay obeisance to you." Gutei was dumbstruck and did not know how to answer. The nun was leaving and Gutei now called to her and asked her to stay with him since it was getting late in the evening. The nun again demanded a turning word. Gutei was once again tongue-tied and the nun left.

Gutei was filled with shame and remorse, and resolved to leave his hut and go in search of a master to train himself properly. During the night he had a dream. The mountain deity appeared in his dream and told him that a master would soon come and help him. So he stayed waiting for the master. A few days later, Master Tenryu visited him. Gutei related events about Jissai and asked the master what turning word he should have given. Tenryu stuck up his finger. With that unexpected gesture, the floodgates of Gutei's mind and heart were opened and he Awakened. All his delusions and dualistic illusions collapsed, and a pure spring wind blew through the entire universe.

Tenryu's one finger is the lotus flower held up by Sakyamuni that led to Mahakashyapa's Enlightenment; it is the pink blossoms of a distant peach tree that Awakened Reiun; it is the sound of a pebble striking a bamboo broom that Awakened Kyogen. Thereafter Gutei's only teaching was to raise his finger. To every question, 'What is the Buddha?', 'Where do you go after death?', 'What is the meaning of life?', Gutei's uplifted finger was the marvellous and inimitable answer. His raised one finger is no-finger; Gutei is not raising his finger, it is his entire Self that comes forth as finger, it is the whole universe; it is, as Mumon says in his commentary, Tenryu, Gutei, the boy and you yourself, all run through with one skewer!

Let's look at the story for its symbolic value. The attendant mimicking the master is our imitative, dualistic, false self. In Zen parlance, it is the self of greed, hatred and illusion. It is the self divided against itself and others, in perpetual fear and anxiety for survival, security and power. It is reactive self, not a free Subject. To free ourselves, we need a conversion, 'a turning of the base'. Zen calls it Great Death. One has to die to oneself, to the false, mimetic self and be born to the True Self that is No-Self.

Such a conversion or transformation cannot be brought about by oneself. In the *koan*, Jissai, meaning true world, comes as the 'other' to Gutei. So also does the 'other' have to enter our world and shatter our illusory cocoon. There is a moving story by Dostoevsky, *The Dream of a Ridiculous Man*, which, briefly put, goes like this: there was once a man who was so withdrawn and depressed, he decided to kill himself. He was about to shoot himself, when he felt a small girl crying and tugging at his sleeve. The man tried to shake her off, but the girl wouldn't let go. So the man consoled her and offered her some help. Comforted, the girl went away. The man went home, determined to kill himself there. He sat down at the table, and took out his revolver, but he found that he was unable to shoot himself. That little girl had broken the barriers of his enclosed self and drawn him out of his self-absorption.

This is what happens when you fall in love: you are transformed, your old self-enclosed, self-sufficient sense of identity is shattered and replaced with a new identity; a new world has opened to you. It is you and yet not you. Your old self has been decentred, recentred and transformed. A new centre, a new depth, has opened in you. More significant than being loved, you are now Awakened as lover. Of course, falling in love is only the opening and breakthrough; it will need lifelong fidelity and generosity for enduring transformation and creativity.

The point here is about the opening. Finite human love is a moment in trans-cosmic love. Taste it even once and there is no going back on the path that has opened up into your heart. You have seen and experienced something new and miraculous and even if you fall into forgetfulness now and then, the memory lingers, giving no peace to your heart. Actually, some primordial memory and trace keeps our unawakened heart restless and searching for its lost home. Are you willing to let unconditional love break into you and break you down? Are you willing to be a lover, and to be the Subject, the Subject beyond all dualities and divisions?

Losing his imitative, false finger, the young boy is Awakened. Gutei lifts up his one finger, the boy looks at his no-finger and Awakens to the reality of No-Self. The story is a stylization that hides the inner drama and complexity. It is not a matter of the finger or no finger, but the Realization of Emptiness, which is the Formless Self. It is the Mystery at the heart of ourselves and of the universe. It is other to us and yet we are not other to it. We are one with it and yet not-one. It cannot be named, yet we have to use some names and symbols.

You die to the old self and Awaken to the Formless Self. 'I alone between heaven and earth.' Or, 'I alone the holy one.' There is a *koan* that goes:

Thousand mountains are covered with snow; why
is one peak not white?

There is not even a speck of dust in the whole heavens; yet, one peak stands out in the Emptiness. Who is that? All the *koans* are about your own self, the True Self, the only Subject in the whole world. Who are you? It is not enough to think you are so-and-so, or such-and-such thing.

When Rabbi Menachem Mendel was a small child, his grandfather, Rabbi Zalman, held him in his lap and asked the child, "Where is Zeide (grandfather)?"

The child touched the grandfather's nose. "No," the rabbi said, "that is Zeide's nose. But where is Zeide?"

The child touched the grandfather's beard. "No, that is Zeide's beard. But where is Zeide?"

The child climbed down, ran to the next room and shouted, "Zeide!" and Rabbi Zalman went into the room.

Gleefully the child pointed, "There is Zeide!"

The message is a powerful one. Zeide is the one who responds when called.

The way you respond and act is the revelation of the Subject that you are. Being and Acting are interdependent and co-inhering. Yet, awareness of being 'I AM' is the ground and root. Awakening is Awakening to being I AM: the Subject, I Alone, Emptiness. This is Gutei's One Finger, I Alone the Holy One.

I particularly like this *koan* for what it tells us about the master-disciple relationship. When Gutei cut off his attendant's finger, was it an act of cruelty or compassion? Since he did it to Awaken the boy, we must assume that it was an act of supreme compassion. Stories such as this abound in Zen Buddhism. Some of the stories may even be apocryphal but they emphasize the unique nature of the master-disciple relationship in Zen. So let's see the coming to birth of this 'I Alone' through 'following' a master. The ideas I present here I take from the book *The Reason of Following* by Robert Scharleman. I give you just the gist to explain my point.

Coming to birth as authentic Self takes place in 'following'. It is both a death and a rebirth. Following is different from all other forms of relating to self and others. 'Following' is the peculiar relationship between master and disciple. The call to follow is to become what one already is. The call, vocation, is from our own inner self. One's own I is presented in the person of the one calling. The call to follow is from the I of I AM to the I of I AM. In the ·ct of following, the one followed is the same as the one following. We follow one whom we can never address as thou but can hear as the I of our own peace or wholeness. A following of the I AM does not lead to the one and the other, the follower and the followed; it leads to the follower's coming to be as I in the fullness of being I. In following, I come to the end of my own despair; I die and am born anew.

Kurtz and Ketcham call this following identification. In their book, *The Spirituality of Imperfection*, they explain: "The disciple, the would-be initiate, approaches the master and says, 'Teach me.' And the teacher replies, 'Come, follow me.' Sometimes, the newcomer tries to insist, 'No, I mean tell me.' And the adept can only smile a welcoming love that cannot be 'told'... Spirituality is a reality that one approaches not by 'learning', but by following. ... learning to be the particular kind of person we are...originates through identification, and identification takes place in community. The question *Who am I?* really asks, 'Where do I belong or fit?' "

Goso said, "When you meet a man on the path who has accomplished the Way, do not greet him with words or silence. Tell me, how will you greet him?"

Hakuin sang:

We meet not knowing each other
We talk not knowing each other's name.

It is not about ordinary human meeting and encounter, it is about meeting the True Self, which is beyond conceptual knowing, beyond all objectifications. It is not a matter of I-Thou relationship, not one of mutuality and trust. It is Awakening to one's own Primal Face: "it is like a man who drinks water and knows for himself whether it is cold or warm." The Awakening to the Original Face, to I AM, incarnated in the fellowship of community, body and earth, is the Realization of 'following'.

A monk asked Joshu, "I have heard that you closely followed Nansen. Is that true?" Joshu said, "Chinsu produces a big radish."

Nansen was Joshu's master; so the question is about Joshu's Realization under Nansen. What was his Realization? Where does he stand now? Where is your master? Who are you? Is it like looking into a mirror and seeing your own face? If it is that, it is nothing but sterile narcissism. Or is it rather the mutual recognition between master and disciple that transforms you and creates history?

> *When Gutei was about to die, he said to the assembled monks, "I received this one-finger Zen from Tenryu. I have used it all my life but have not exhausted it." Having said this,* the koan ends, *"he entered Nirvana."*

How do you realize the inexhaustible one-finger Zen? Do you lift up your finger? It needs to be chopped off!

Thousand Mistakes, Ten Thousand Mistakes

Unmon said, "The world is vast and wide like this. Why do you put on your seven-panel robe at the sound of the bell?"

Unmon was a disciple of Seppo and belonged to the 10th century. He was eloquent with words, but at the same time mistrusted them. Unmon was what you would call an iconoclast. In one of his sermons to his assembly, he related this legend about the birth of the Buddha: it is said that immediately after his birth, the Buddha took seven steps, looked at the four quarters, and with one hand pointing to the heavens and the other pointing to the earth, declared, "Above heaven and below earth, I alone am the Honoured One." Unmon related this story and then said, "If I had been a witness to this scene, I would have knocked him to death with a single stroke and given his flesh to dogs for food. This would have been my contribution to the peace and harmony of the world."

The world is vast and wide like this: all is empty, there is not even a speck of dust or obstruction. Everything interpenetrates with everything else. It is Indra's net of diamonds: each diamond reflects and holds within it the entire universe.

Unmon asked a monk, "An old man said, 'In the realm of nondualism there is not the slightest obstacle

> between self and other.' What about Japan and Korea in this context?" The monk said, "They are not different." The Master remarked, "You go to hell."
>
> A monk asked Unmon, "Who is my Self?" Unmon answered, "The one who roams freely in the mountains and takes his delight in the streams."

Unmon asks the monks why, at the sound of the bell, they immediately put on their robes and go to attend to whatever task the bell beckons them. Why do they follow the call of the bell? The seven-panel robe here refers to an outer robe made of seven strips of cloth; this is one of the three robes of a monk. The nine-strip robe was the most ceremonious one, the five-strip one the simplest. The seven-strip one was probably used to attend the formal talks of the master. In a monastery, the bell punctuates and marks the different functions and tasks of the day; it is a call and a sign. Now Unmon asks his monks, at the sound of the bell you choose to put on the robe, at the sound of the bell you choose to go to the talk: why?

This is a question we can address to ourselves. In the place of the monk's bell we can assume maybe the ringing of the telephone; the call of someone; the call to work; or something of greater importance like choosing a partner, choosing a job. We are answering all the time, we cannot escape choices. We do it all our waking hours. Even not to answer is an answer, a choice we are making. At the heart of reality lies indetermination and choice. The present and the future are possibilities, and we are given the choice of bringing into actuality the one or the other possibility. In this, our freedom lies more in the attitude we take than in action. Action follows within the parameters of our body, mind, society and nature. However, for what reasons do we choose? Why?

The Why asks for our reasons, and for the causes. It asks the question about our free will and choice. Have we freedom of choice? What sort of freedom is it? And when we choose, for what reasons do we do so? We would like to believe that we are totally free to choose as we like; that nothing can take away this freedom of ours, that our dignity lies in this causeless, unconditioned, unstructured freedom; that our self is freedom itself, suspended in mid-air.

This is a mistaken belief. There is no individual I standing over and against the world. Oneness and solidarity with the world is our true basic condition. Trust in Being and Compassion for the world and self is our true way of being. There is no unconditioned or unstructured choice; our body and heart are already set on some chosen path prior to our reflexive awareness; we come to reflexive awareness in order to clarify, confirm and own up the heart's choice: there is compassion and caring along with letting-be, there is address and responsibility: it is a call and response to the call.

A monk, Seizei, once eagerly asked Master Sozan,
"I am solitary and destitute. I beg you, Master, please
help me become prosperous."
Sozan said, "Venerable Seizei!"
"Yes, Master," replied Seizei.
Sozan said, "You have already drunk three cups of
the fine Hakka wine and still you say that you have
not yet moistened your lips."

There is a time when you 'die' to yourself—a time when you let go everything, experience the void, and surrender yourself. From such experience you come to resurrection—come to new life, experience self and world anew, come to a new vision of a new world. This new vision and new life are in terms of the transcendental values of Being, Oneness, Goodness, Truth, Justice and Beauty. These are not totally new; for your heart was from the beginning Buddha-nature. But it was clouded, distorted, repressed, and inchoate. Now the heart is liberated and transformed—converted and Awakened—and it lives in the light and power of the Transcendental Values.

The measure and the way one lives these is unique to the individual. The light comes refracted through the prism of each individual and the way one experiences it is one's own secret and mystery. Even to say that there is someone experiencing and thinking of it, as if the experiencer and the experience are two, may be wrong. It is the way of being oneself; the 'essence', the ground plan, of one's existence and being. To be true to this way of being is to be in transcendental trust and caring, which is a form of letting-be: letting Being/Truth/Goodness come forth, be revealed; or as the poet T S Eliot puts it, "Teach us to care and not to care."

There is no 'why' one feels and cares, no 'why' one responds. The heart feels touched and it responds. Being calls, Truth and Justice call, Goodness touches and calls. When you respond, in compassion, your heart experiences peace, joy, freedom. It is in experiencing the peace, joy and freedom that you know you are 'on the Way'. "Though the Way of the Awakened is unsurpassed, I vow to walk along all the Way," goes the bodhisattva vow. You walk along in the dark, guided by the light of the heart; now stumbling, now wandering yet always moving on the right path. It is in a sense not so much I who move: it is Emptiness that moves, it is the whole universe that moves. There is moving in not-moving. Just keep on moving, walk on. No 'whys', no reasons, no explanations.

Mountains echo
To the sound of temple bells
In the moonlight.

In the world of Emptiness, there is nothing and nobody; there is no choice, no words, and no non-words. But you cannot 'live' in Emptiness; there is no power in it to save the world if you are attached to Emptiness. Or to put it in another way, true Emptiness is actualized and embodied in Compassion. If it is not embodied thus, it is only illusion. You are called, you respond. It is in being called and in responding that you realize the No-Self. Master Rinzai says on ascending the rostrum to preach: "Today, having found it impossible to refuse, I have complied with people's wishes and stepped up to the lecture seat. If I were to discuss the great concern of Buddhism from the point of view of a follower of the sect of the Ch'an patriarchs, then I could not even open my mouth, and you would have no place to plant your feet. But today I have been urged to speak by the Constant Attendant, so why should I hide the principles of our sect?"

You step out of the hundred foot pole, get out of 'sitting in' Emptiness and enter the marketplace of the world, the world of duality. To the Awakened person, it is neither duality, nor non-duality. You Awaken to the world as your very self. The world is yourself and you are the world. Forget yourself and respond to the call here and now. Acting means to make mistakes, to take responsibility, to commit yourself. In *Zen Flesh, Zen Bones* by Paul Reps, there is a story titled *Eating the Blame*. A cook in a Zen monastery cuts some green vegetables from the garden and chops them up and prepares the soup, unaware that in his haste he had included a part of a snake in the vegetables. The master and the monks enjoy the soup. But when the master finds the snake's head in his bowl, he summons the cook. "What is this?" he demands, holding up the head of the snake. "Oh, thank you, master," replies the cook, taking the morsel and eating it quickly. To respond, to act, is to commit yourself; to act and to commit yourself is 'to make a mistake'—it is the 'mistake' of letting go attachment to stillness and Emptiness, and falling into *samsara*, the world of illusions. 'As soon as you step out of the monastery, there is grass; nay, grass is everywhere.' The Enlightened person 'goes straight ahead and journeys deep into the recesses of the hundred thousand mountains'—as you know, grass and mountains here are delusions and illusions of the world. Alas, your whole life is one mistake.

> *Not falling, not obscuring,*
> *Two faces, one die.*
> *Not obscuring, not falling,*
> *A thousand mistakes, ten thousand mistakes.*

says a verse of Mumon's.

When you have given up your attachment to Buddhas and Patriarchs, Enlightenment and Emptiness, gain and loss, you are freed to live this life wholeheartedly. You can live in the Now and flow with the circumstances. Then everything becomes grace even while all is a mistake. It is blowing with the wind, swimming with the stream:

"When the wind blows through the willows, the downy seed-balls float away; when the rain beats on the pear blossoms, a butterfly flies away."

It is wholeheartedly living and acting, with all of your vulnerabilities, uncertainties and weaknesses. In tenderness, compassion, humility, courage and forgiveness. This way is not a blind way, but one of discernment and understanding. You respond according to circumstances and times, in accordance with your heart-mind that abides in the Transcendental Values. To a swordsman, give a sword, to a child something else. This you learn by experience, by listening to your heart-mind as well as listening to the one calling. Often you will have to practise a sort of 'epoche', a 'bracketing' of your prejudices and ideas and listen. Of course, you cannot completely stand outside of all your pre-judgements and views; yet this will be your practice, 'to empty' yourself again and again, to listen in loving attentiveness and respond compassionately. It is also important to remember that your thoughts and emotions are not the causes forcing you to act on them. Do not become a slave of your emotions and thoughts. Do not be used by the 24 hours but use them, as Rinzai would say.

> *A monk asked Unmon, "Who is my Self?" Unmon answered, "The one who roams freely in the mountains and takes his delight in the streams."*

Writes Mumon,

> *The great Way has no gates,*
> *Thousands of paths enter it;*
> *When you pass through this gateless gate,*
> *You walk freely between heaven and earth.*

Such freedom is a gift. When you have let go all attachments; when you have faced and experienced your own impermanence, death and extinction as well as that of the others; when you have fallen through the void and are resurrected to Emptiness that is graciousness; when you have touched the bottom of your neediness and vulnerability and experienced mercy and compassion: then are born freedom and compassion.

> *Joshu addressed the assembly: "The real Way is not difficult. It only abhors choice and attachment. With but a single word there may arise choice and attachment or there may arise clarity. This old monk does not have that clarity. Do you appreciate the meaning of this or not?" A monk asked, "If you do not have that clarity, what do you appreciate?" Joshu said, "I do not know that, either." The monk said,*

"If you do not know, how can you say you do not have that clarity?" Joshu said, "Asking the question is good enough. Now make your bows and retire."

Now tell me, how do you realize the real Way that is beyond choice and attachment? How will you go beyond your ego-self and act wholeheartedly, in freedom and compassion? Who is that who acts thus?

Unmon and the Sickness of the World

Unmon said to his disciples, "Medicine and sickness cure each other. All the earth is medicine. Where do you find yourself?"

There are other *koans* of Unmon somewhat similar to this one:
Unmon spoke to his assembly and said, "Everybody has his own light. If he tries to see it, everything is darkness. What is everybody's light?"

And again, he said,
Blessing things cannot be better than nothing.

What is the cure for your illness? Buddhism holds that human illness is basically illusion, and from illusion are born greed and hatred. Unmon says all the earth is medicine. There is a story in *Kidogoroku, The 100 koans of Master Kido,* that goes:

Manjusri once asked Zenzai, an earnest Zen student, to bring him something that was not medicine. Zenzai could find nothing that could not work as a medicine. Manjusri then asked him to bring something that was definitely a medicine. Zenzai handed Manjusri a blade of grass. Manjusri held it up and said to his assembly, "This single blade of grass can give life to a man and can also bring death to him."

The Self is Emptiness, a no-thing. It is boundless openness, so to say. There is no going and coming in it; it is vast darkness, beyond the ken of human intellect. It is a no-thing, an empty hole; you cannot grasp it.

This Emptiness is our freedom, but failing to understand that, we try to hold on to ourselves through filling ourselves with a myriad diversions and activities. We do not want to acknowledge our human condition of finitude and mortality. But we cannot escape it, for everything and everyone comes with the message, 'we too will pass away'.

We are frustrated with other human beings and the world's goods, for they fail to fulfil our neediness and demands. It is our ego-assertion and narcissism that cause our suffering. The suffering of others becomes unbearable, often more so than our own. We cling to our illusions, we construct fantasy worlds, we pray and cry to be saved from our terrors and sufferings; we even lash at the others who by their sufferings have drawn us into suffering. René Girard has called the mimetic or imitative desire of greed as the root cause of human illness and violence; our desire for fulfilment of the self in some object or other through imitation and rivalry of others pulls us into a vortex of greed and violence. What is the cure for this illness? The great Master Unmon says, all the world is medicine. There is medicine, but how do we take it? If taken wrongly, it can become poison. Nagarjuna says that Emptiness is like a poisonous snake, which when taken hold of wrongly can be death.

The Zen way to liberation enfolds Awakening and Compassion. Let me briefly touch upon the first. When we have gone deep into the midst of darkness and Emptiness, in the night that is darker than night, in the loneliness and 'lostness' even as we are accompanied by an other, if we let ourselves go and surrender ourselves into that Emptiness, and die the Great Death so to say, then light dawns on us. The darkness is light, the Emptiness is graciousness. We Awaken to Emptiness as our ground and nature. In renouncing and letting go all our attachments to the ego's objects of desire for salvation, whether it is god, Nirvana, world or self, we become transformed and liberated. We realize we are embraced in unconditional love; we are love, our self is all the world. We have nowhere to stand on and that is our home!

"The inexhaustible fullness of nothingness; flowers bloom, the moon shines."

Emptiness that is graciousness! The whole universe is a manifestation of Emptiness. Emptiness, to use another word, is Mystery/*Mysterion;* it is also openness as well as opening; it is letting-be. Emptiness is the in-between of I and Thou as well as the Beyond-Within that lets-be the I and Thou. It is Emptiness that makes possible our encounter and meeting. In short, liberation and salvation are in the Realization of Emptiness that is Mystery, Mystery that is graciousness.

This is the 'turning of the base', the great Death and great Awakening. But the journey is not yet complete—it is completed only in the return to the marketplace of the world, to the human others and the non-human world. We find life, 'come home' and are healed truly only when we realize the other and the world as our very self. Mountains and rivers, the blade of grass and the piece of tile, are but our own self that is Emptiness. We 'empty' ourselves, so to say, and let-be mountains and rivers, the blade of grass and the piece of tile. We are a clearing for the world to come to be. The world is our self. The 'I' is now the sound of the birds, falling of leaves, barking dogs and grazing cows. In this, the face of the human other has a unique place; it touches and transforms our hearts, it becomes our very heart and soul. It is the face of Emptiness greeting us and making its home in us.

Mahakaruna, Great Compassion, is the Realization of the other and the world as our very self. It is letting the other be the other and it is letting the other be as our own self. It is openness to the other/world; it is letting-be, *wu-wei* or action in non-action. It is letting-be the other, experiencing the other, and caring for the other that heals and makes one whole. It is to love the other as yourself, for the other is your self. Your heart and mind are an openness and space for the other and the world. When the other and the world are yourself, then your self is the world/others. Mountains, rivers and the wide earth are nothing but your self. The world is your self and the self is the world.

Most Zen students are familiar with this *koan*, which is in four parts:

In the sea of Ise, ten thousand feet down, lies a single stone; I wish to pick up that stone without wetting my hands.
On the stone a name is inscribed; what is the name?
On one side of the name it reads, 'Cannot get wet'.
On the other side of the name it reads, 'Cannot get dry'.

What is that marvellous stone? How can you get it without wetting your hands? What do 'wetting' and 'not wetting' or 'being ever dry' mean? The stone is, of course, your True Self. The first statement or question calls you to realize your True Self. The others clarify what is involved in realizing the True Self. Let me explain the meaning a little. 'Cannot get wet' means that your True Self is beyond all dualities and particularities; beyond all passion, suffering, divisions, definitions, attachments, relations. In short, totally empty, abiding nowhere. 'Cannot get dry' means that the Self is, paradoxically, always in suffering, passion, dualities, attachments. The *koan* as a whole tells us that the True

Self is at once empty and full of compassion. 'Cannot get dry' also means that the tears of compassion cannot be dried.

As the Mahayana/Zen saying goes, the bodhisattva sees there is nobody to be saved and labours ceaselessly to save all beings!

Zen usually makes use of the natural world, the world of mountains, rivers, trees and so on to point to the true nature of things. In the practice of *koans*, 'contemplation of nature' gives one a non-threatening space 'to be'. But our practice is, above all, with the human world; and it has a special place with the neighbour and the stranger. True, Great Compassion embraces all beings, rich and poor, good and bad, sinner and saint, animal and human, trees and stones. Yet, compassion has a natural affinity with and proximity to the poor and the suffering. True compassion is to stand in their place, and to experience their humanity and mystery; to experience their beauty and worth, strength and dignity, their pain and sorrow, vulnerability and mortality. It is to know your kinship with them; to laugh with them and to cry with them, and to be deeply moved by mercy and compassion. It is mercy and compassion that transform you and heal you. Compassion means *cum+passio*, suffering-with. However, compassion does not mean sharing only in suffering and pain. It is also being touched by the goodness of others. It is in being so touched by others' goodness and mercy that you feel liberated. In compassion, the distance between you and the other is crossed. Compassion actualizes the non-duality of self and other. Compassion is the true face of selflessness. In compassion the other and the world are realized as your very self. And by losing your self you find yourself. It is a continuous, ongoing call to actualization.

Compassion leads to action with and for the other and the world. Compassion is the motive for ethical action. It is the vulnerable face of the other that touches your heart and calls you forth. The 'I' comes forth in being touched and called forth by the other/world. But the focus here is not the 'I'; the 'I' is forgotten, emptied. However, self and other, self and world, are brought forth in compassion. In loving the other and the world, the self is loved.

Avalokiteshvara (Kanzeon or Kannon in Japanese) is the bodhisattva or Buddhist ideal of compassion and mercy, whose very being is the hearing of the cries of the beings of the world and becoming one body of compassion. At our Zen centre here we recite the Heart Sutra everyday—in this *sutra*, Avalokiteshvara realizes the Emptiness of self and beings and thus becomes the bodhisattva of compassion. Emptiness and compassion, *prajna* and *karuna*, are the two sides of one Realization. One without the other is not authentic and complete.

Zen Awakening opens into compassion. The face of the other, the cry of the world, breaks open your heart and thus you realize the no-self which is not apart from the others and the world. But in the world of institutions and laws, society has to deal with matters of rights, obligations and justice. Justice and rights are necessary dimensions of the world we live in. People have to struggle for justice and rights. With justice and rights, power becomes fundamental and basic. To live in the world is to deal with power. In the Awakened way, however, justice is in reality Great Compassion.

The justice of the world is distributive justice. Justice and rights, and the use of power, come first from the struggle for survival and the dignity of human living; and then it leads inevitably to comparisons and demands fuelled by the spiralling of what Girard calls imitative desires. More often than not, the talk of justice and rights becomes a matter of demands for equality and power leading to confrontation, combativeness, division and defensiveness;

violence is inescapable in all of this. It is competition and struggle, fear and hostility. Power has become the master.

In the Zen way of Awakening and Compassion, there is no more the dualism of self and other. The world is the self; mercy and compassion bind us together. Being here and now and being-with the others/world, letting-be and suffering-with, is the way of being self. The pain of the other becomes your own pain and you seek to alleviate it. It is like a baby crying on hearing the cry of another baby, a 'contagion of cries'. The feeling of pity springs from our inmost self. The so-called enemy is not an alien but our own self. Compassion is instinctive and natural but it also demands conversion from narcissism. Justice, life-giving justice, flows from compassion; whereas compassion cannot flow from justice and rights; this is the sickness of the world, where the fight for justice and rights has become primary and the world is becoming heartless. In compassion and mercy, there is abundance for all the world, overflowing and super-abounding. We need justice but it needs to flow from compassion.

I do not mean to sound like a dreamer wishing up some utopia. Let me 'get real' as they say. All injustices cannot be done away with, nor can all sorrow and suffering be wiped off the face of the earth. So what is the place of compassion? As I said earlier, compassion is primarily a way of being, being-with, suffering-with. In the midst of our caring and doing, we face the intractability of life, of illness, old age and death, of the failures of nature and of oneself and others. We face and suffer our intractability and the perversity, the impossibility of doing away with injustice and wars. Our abilities and capacities are limited; we have to renounce our fantasies and programmes. We find ourselves often impotent before the causes of misfortune and misdeeds. We are called to suffer in patience; it is a sorrowful yet hope-filled patience. It is not resignation, not despair.

Let me end with another *koan* from Master Unmon. It may sound contrary to what has been said earlier and seem even to take you away from compassion. But paradoxically, the *koan* goes to the heart of the matter and challenges you to the actualization of great Awakening and great compassion simultaneously:

> *Unmon addressed the assembly and said, "I am not asking you about the days before the fifteenth of the month. But what about after the fifteenth? Come and give me a word about those days." And he himself gave the answer for them: "Every day is a good day."*

'Good' here is not the ordinary good in contrast to the bad. How do you realize this Good in the midst of the suffering and evil in the world? How?

> *Kyozan asked Sansho, "What is your name?"*

Child of Emptiness

Sansho said, "Ejaku!"
Kyozan said, "Ejaku is my name!"
Sansho said, "My name is Enen!"
Kyozan laughed heartily.

Kyozan, who lived in the 9th century in China, was a disciple of Isan. He and Isan jointly established the Igyo school, one of the five schools of Zen in China. Sansho was Rinzai's disciple and succeeded him. Here, the two of them meet and this exchange follows.

Kyozan of course knew Sansho's name, but we must remember that this is a Zen encounter. When asked his name, Sansho takes Kyozan's name, Ejaku. This was Kyozan's personal name. When Kyozan protests that it is his name ("Ejaku is my name"), Sansho takes his own name ("My name is Enen"). Upon which Kyozan laughs.

Is this Zen craziness or Zen Enlightenment? What's going on here? Setcho, the commentator of *Hekiganroku*, sees in this exchange a staging of the Zen ideas of grasping and releasing. Or, in other Zen terms, it is killing and giving life. Who are you, asks Kyozan. Sansho answers, I am you. This may remind you of the Sufi story: the lover comes and knocks at the door of the beloved. The voice from within asks, who is it? The lover answers, this is so-and-so. The answer comes, go away, I do not know you! The lover knocks again, and again the question comes, who is it? The lover answers, I am you! The door opens in welcome.

What is happening in this story and in our Zen encounter is paradigmatic of becoming of oneself through mutual recognition. One comes to the fullness of oneself only through the other's recognition and affirmation. Hegel articulates this process beautifully: the self-consciousness of the first is reflected in the second; the first sees the self mirrored in the other and in this mirroring recognizes herself/himself. In this phase, the other has, in a sense, disappeared and only Self is seen.

This mirroring at the same time leads the mirrored one to return to herself/himself. In this returning, one releases the other to be the other. This is not a one-way process, but a mutual recognition and mutual affirmation. In being recognized, one also offers recognition to the other. Each recognizes oneself in the other and lets the other be the other in returning to oneself. This takes place not only between grown-up people, it is thus from the very beginning of human birth, beginning with the relationship between mother and child. Being comes to birth in the in-between of I and Thou, in mutual recognition and affirmation. As Hegel puts it, "Each (self-consciousness) is for the other the middle term, through which each mediates itself with itself and unites with itself." However, the other is not the cause of the self and self-consciousness. The other is the call of the Self to authenticity and truth, and to Awakening. With Awakening, one comes to realize the other as oneself.

It is desire that drives one to seek recognition from the other and thus 'beg' for space to exist, to be oneself. Heart calls to Heart. Desire is fulfilled in the recognition and the returning to oneself in self-consciousness. But since desire was for the other, even though desire is fulfilled in the return to oneself, the original direction of desire goes on endlessly. This desire seeks further and further fulfilment—to its own doom. The human heart and mind, with its potential to open itself to the infinite, can never be completely fulfilled by other humans or finite things of the world. Desire is both satisfied and can never be satisfied. The heart-mind has to be reformed and transformed. It has to become desireless desire for the other, a desire that is not a self-centred need and want. If not, desire becomes distorted, becomes a matter of power struggle and pans out in the deluded ways of societies, cultures and individuals.

How is all this reflected in the 'naming' *koan*? Sansho's answer to Kyozan taking Kyozan's own name ("Ejaku") is usually seen as Sansho taking away Kyozan's identity. It can be seen differently. With his question, ("What is your name?") Kyozan seeks himself in the other. Kyozan does not yet recognize Sansho in his otherness; he seeks only to impose himself on the other. Sansho then mirrors Kyozan to Kyozan ("Ejaku"). Kyozan returns to himself in that recognition and in the process releases Sansho to Sansho ("Ejaku is my name"). Sansho then releases Kyozan to Kyozan by taking up his own identity ("My name is Enen"). It is Kyozan's desire—pretended or not— which brings about the dance of mutual recognition and release. Kyozan's laughter displays the joy and marvel of this dance.

This is a beautiful *koan*, apparently nonsensical but very deep in the articulation of its protagonists' Enlightenment. The playfulness of the encounter between two Enlightened masters is quintessential Zen. There is a lot of playfulness and fun in Zen practice, especially *koan* practice.

This encounter, of course, displays both the human predicament and the joyful freedom of the Awakened ones from the predicament. One comes to freedom and fulfilment of desire through mutual recognition and affirmation. But desire is endless and our security is never secure enough. We face the contingencies of life—its finitude, mortality, suffering and darkness, meaninglessness, void, evil, guilt, responsibility—and we find it unbearable and unsolvable. Actually, the mutual recognition and the in-between of humans open us to a fathomless abyss and darkness. There is only one way out, and that is conversion: a letting-go and falling into the abyss, and in that fall, being embraced by Emptiness and Mystery that is graciousness. It is Awakening to Emptiness and realizing oneself as Emptiness. Your true Father is Emptiness! You are the child of Emptiness, nay, you are Emptiness. Emptiness is the Self, the Self is Emptiness. Emptiness is your Father and you are Emptiness—both are true!

The Self is not your ego-self; but the ego-self is not apart from the Self. In the words of Jesus, "My Father and I are one." And, "I am in the Father and the Father is in me." In the beautiful words of John Dunne: "The sense of I, located in the moving centre of life, is the place where the other world passes through this world, where the eternal enters time in us, where the human figure emerges and then returns to its divine ground. It is a place where god comes into the world and where the world comes back to god." This is not merely or only my 'I'; it embraces and includes I, You, We and all of the world.

There is a story of a devotee of Lord Krishna: the devotee was beaten up and severly wounded by dacoits; some passers-by took pity on the wounded man lying in the ditch at night, dressed him and cared for him. When he came to himself and was asked what had happened, the devotee replied, "Krishna came and beat me up; now Krishna comes and dresses my wounds and cares for me. What a play my Krishna is playing with me!" It is a beautiful story of devotion and faith. However, for the Awakened person who transcends devotion and faith it will be: Krishna is the one who wounds and who heals; Krishna is the one who is wounded and who is healed. It is in action, above all, that the Self is manifested and revealed. *Standing nowhere, the mind comes forth.* How do you come forth? Who is that who comes forth? And from where?

The Buddha is said to have exclaimed in ecstatic joy: "There exists, monks, that in which there is no birth, where nothing has come into existence, where nothing has been made, where there is nothing conditioned. If that in which there is no birth... did not exist, no escape here from what is born, become, made conditioned would be known. But since there is that in which there is no birth, where nothing has come into existence, where nothing has been made, where there is nothing conditioned, an escape here for what is born, become, made, conditioned is known."

The Unconditioned is the ground of your being and selfhood; it is your Father and Mother; and it is your very Self. The Buddha did not use words like 'Father' or 'Mother', neither will Zen use these personal words. We have to be reticent in our use of such terms; however, without such terms and images, our experience will be stunted and stifled. We have to negate all terms of ultimate correspondence and truth and at the same time be freed to move and dwell in images and symbols, particularly personal symbols and images. Kill the Buddha if you meet him on the way; and at the same time, as Huang-po teaches by personal example, make prostrations to the Buddha freely. This Reality of our Original Face is beyond all names and forms. "Here, thought, feeling, knowledge and imagination are of no avail," sings Seng-ts'an in *On Believing in the Mind.*

Reality is both *is* and *is-not*; it is personal and transpersonal; it is not-one and not-two. This not-two and not-one applies in a particular way to the relationship between the Self and the ego-self. Madhyamika logic extends this not-two, not-one further: everything is suchness; everything is not suchness; everything is both suchness and not suchness; and, everything is neither suchness nor not suchness.

Ultimate Reality both includes and is beyond all such terms. It is mystery, unknowing. At the same time, it is the inmost of your inmost self. It is by becoming 'at-oned' with this Self that is Emptiness, which is beyond all names and forms, which is not simply your ego-self and yet which is the ground of your ego-self, that liberation is realized, salvation attained. Then the Self has become the Subject that is yourself. This Self is not apart from the world. Your imagination and emotions have to be purified and freed to 'receive' all the world and to stand in the place of each and every being. It is to be and let-be; to act and respond and thus to be a home for the other and to come home to oneself.

The mutual recognition and affirmation we mentioned as the beginning and confirmation of human selfhood is the door to this ultimate ground of reality as well as the celebration of it. In Awakening, desire and vision have been de-structured, transformed and re-formed. Each and every thing and person becomes the manifestation, revelation, of the Reality. It is manifested in the in-between of dialogue and encounter. This in-between of dialogue flows from and embraces Emptiness itself, which is realized in terms of self-emptying and letting the other be. You can call it deep empathy; but it flows from the ground where you and the other, you and the world, are one and not-one. Meister Eckhart explains it thus: "There may be water in a tub, and the tub surrounds it, but where the wood is, there is no water. In this sense no material thing dwells in another, but every spiritual thing does dwell in another. Every single angel is in the next with all his joy, with all his happiness and all his beatitude as perfectly as in himself; and every angel with all his joy and all his beatitude is in me, and so is God Himself with all his beatitude, though I know it not."

Roger Corless, from whose essay *Many Selves, Many Realities* I got the above quotation, calls this mutual co-inherence. This term is a translation of the Greek term *perichoresis*, which is used in Christian theology to describe the Christian god of the Trinity: the Father, the Son and the Spirit, each indwelling in the other in a sort of eternal dance. The danger in the use of this language is that the ego-self can appropriate this image to itself, as though the ego-self is the eternal partner with god. This then becomes the illusion of ego inflation! The ego-self has to lose itself in order to find itself. It is only with this that the *koan* of Kyozan and Sansho comes to full clarity. "My name is Ejaku", says Sansho. He has emptied himself and let Kyozan stand in his place. He finds his identity through Kyozan. It is the same for Kyozan. The ego-self realizes itself in Emptiness in its opening to the other and the world. But in actuality it is the Self that is openness to the other and the world, the Self that is already the other and the world. What is already the Reality is realized and actualized in the actual calling and responding, in being and letting-be the other. Thus it takes place not simply in some inner experience or in the mind, or in some kind of thought, but in terms of dialogue and conversation, response and action. You, the Self, are now 'I', now 'Thou'; now 'self and other forgotten: nothing at all'; or now 'the cypress tree in the courtyard'—each time it is 'I Alone'. Your imagination and emotion have to be transformed and freed, but they have to bear fruit in action and dialogue. It is in one's way of being and attitude as well as in one's response and action that the Self that is No-Self is actualized. When our hearts are grounded in Emptiness, each and everything can become the revelation and call of Emptiness, freeing us further into peace, freedom and joy. Each event, each thing, is a call and address. It is the Self calling, the Self answering.

Have you heard of the 'Perfect Joy of St. Francis'? Here is the story: one day Francis asked brother Leo if he knew what true joy was. Francis himself answered, saying first that even if all the great and learned people joined the Order of Francis, it will not be perfect joy. He continued:

"But what is true joy? I am returning from Perugia and I am coming here at night, in the dark. It is wintertime and wet and muddy and so cold that icicles form at the edges of my habit and keep striking my legs and blood flows from such wounds. And I come to the gate, all covered with mud and cold and ice, and after I have knocked and called for a long time, a friar comes and asks, 'Who are you?' I answer, 'Brother Francis.' And he says, 'Go away. This is not a decent time to be going about. You can't come in.' And when I insist again, he replies, 'Go away. You are a simple and uneducated fellow. From now on don't stay with us any more. We are so many and so important that we don't need you.' But I still stand at the gate and say, 'For the love of god, let me in tonight.' And he answers, 'I won't. Go to the Crosiers' place and ask there.'

"I tell you that if I kept patience and was not upset—that is true joy and true virtue and the salvation of the soul."

What was the mind and heart of Francis like in this? Can you see that there is no resentment, no bitterness, no blaming? There is only peace, compassion and joy. He is not a victim, he will not play the victim game. He is the Master, the Subject that is Freedom and Compassion. It means, in Christian terms, Francis has 'come home' to his god as his abiding ground. He has become 'oned' with Christ. The friar who rejects and sends him away is none but Christ himself. Francis' heart's desire and mind's vision have been de-structured, broken through and transformed. Hence his heart and mind are open to all the world. His heart is not only an openness, but also is peace, peace with all the world. Only when your heart and mind have come to abide in 'the peace which the world cannot give', can they be open without reserve to others and the world.

How do you come to that peace? Where do you find true joy? Joshu asks you in a *koan*,

Is the Subject in?

How do you Awaken to the Self that is the Subject? What sort of Subject? It is a question about your vision and attitude, your way of being and responding. Who you are can be realized only in the in-between of call and response. You are called and addressed all the time. And you, too, ask the other/the world, *Who am I?* and *Who are you?*

Part II

If Not Now, When?

If Not Now, When?

To live a life of Zen is to live in the mysticism of the now, of the particular and concrete. What does this living in the now mean? It is as simple as Zen Enlightenment: the now is the now! We live in the now, everything flows through the now, we cannot jump out of the now. Jesus said, "Look at the lilies of the field, and the birds of the air; do not be anxious for tomorrow, tomorrow will take care of itself." A Christian spiritual master, Jean de Caussade, talked of the Sacrament of the Now. He said, you cannot touch god or Reality except in the now of your living. He talked of Abandonment or Surrender to god in the Now. Do not seek god somewhere else. Just be present, be aware, respond to life as it comes to you Here and Now.

Simple, isn't it? Yet this apparent simplicity is full of traps and pitfalls. They appear when living in the present becomes a means of indulging our ego-self. Living in the Now becomes, for many of us, the philosophy of Carpe Diem: enjoy the day as long as it lasts. I don't need to stress that this is completely counterproductive.

You can enter the Now only as a free and conscious Subject. This involves taking responsibility for yourself, learning to accept your desires and not live by the desires and expectations of others. It is only by being true to yourself, to your heart's desires and decisions, and taking responsibility for yourself that you become yourself and begin to live truly. In this process, the images of god as a super other standing over and against you have to go. God has to die.

On the other hand, becoming oneself as a free subject involves meeting the human other as other. All of this is part of the process of self-becoming. It is a process that leads to being open to the infinite, as an emptiness that can never be controlled, comprehended or closed. It is an openness and mystery coming into existence without end through surrender, from the inmost centre of one's being, into the Mystery of love. It is the transformation that comes from losing oneself and discovering oneself as 'I AM' and 'I AM LOVE'. This Self embraces all the world and yet comes to be only through the narrow door of the Here and the Now.

The verse *On Believing in the Mind* by the Third Patriarch of Zen in China ends with these words:

The Way is beyond language, for in it there is
no yesterday
no tomorrow
no today.

Only when you have touched the beyond-of-time, only when you have experienced Eternity, can you come to live in and appreciate time and history. We humans live in time as well as in Eternity. Eternity is not apart from time and history. Time is but the rainbow of Eternity. Space is often used as a symbol for Nirvana; for space is without bounds, all are present in space simultaneously; space is pure and not sullied by the things of the world. We humans are stretched between the past and the future and long for what is not, as the poet says. Time is not a linear, one-dimensional reality. The past is with us Here and Now, we are what we have been. All the past is gathered up in us and is here and now. The future is not somewhere in the far away. It is in the Here and Now, influencing us in terms of our hopes, dreams, longings and fears. Our selves are stretched between the past and the future, in memory and hope, fear and longing, guilt and responsibility. The future is not simply in front of us; it comes from our hidden, unknown depths; the past dwells in our depths too. The depths are beyond our complete comprehension. We live out of the depths, but the depths also well up and confront us. All conscious action is movement, movement forward, which is towards the future or towards possibilities; this is to live and to love in response and responsibility. You are called, you respond.

Since the past and the future are in the Now, we can also change and reshape them. The past comes to us in memory and imagination. It is through the imagination, driven by the heart's longings, that we dwell in the past and the future even as we live in the Now. Thus, we can re-shape and re-envision our past through imagination. The past is to be seen anew and re-fashioned, forgiven and accepted in gratitude. The future can be received in trusting openness and hope. Past memories need to be healed, forgiven, or celebrated and the future anticipated in joy and trust. We live and move not in the so-called brute facts, but in memory, imagination and emotion. Humans are interpreting animals and we are beings of imitative desires. We create and re-create, tell and re-tell the reality of our selves, others and the world in imaginative narrative and story. Myths, metaphors, symbols and language are our clothing and the expression of our desires, passions, loves and visions. Memory and imagination are the powers of the heart for creation and re-creation.

Reality is greater than our individual ego-self. We normally experience reality and the world through our bounded ego-selves. But our self is not merely bound within the individual skin and body. Our self dwells in the in-between of self and others. I am not I except in relaiton to others.

Each of us is interdependent. Our identity is not a closed identity, closed in on oneself; it is an open identity. It is through meeting others, in dialogue and exchange, that we become ourselves. More, we are basically an openness—only by actualizing this openness again and again, can we be true to ourselves, be authentic. I, the person, the Subject, am the entire universe; the universe comes forth as the I, the Subject. At the same time, it is in this body, in this heart-mind, in this locus, that I live and realize reality and truth. The True Self is not apart from this body-mind-heart self, but shines forth as Subject, as I.

Reality is Here and Now. But it is in many layers, many dimensions, many forms, many kinds—depth upon depth, layer upon layer, one going through the other. Our mind cannot comprehend all of it. It is full of paradoxes, contradictions, ambiguities, indeterminacies; it is partly revealed and partly hidden, transparent yet mysterious. We are in the midst of an ever-flowing stream; we are flowing with the stream and we are the stream. Religions talk of heaven and hell, of life-after-life. There is only this life, in its many layers and many depths. There is only Now. Now, of course, is not a point of time—it is a way of being present to ourselves and others and the world; being aware, accepting to live life to the full, responding to the call of love and life.

Religious traditions and rituals fulfil certain needs and functions. But religious dogmas and doctrines are not to be taken literally. Literalism kills the spirit. The myths and symbols, stories and parables of the different religions have been given to us to console, guide, open up and enrich our imagination and emotions. Unfortunately, people too often take dogmas, beliefs and doctrines to be literal truths. They then become blind to life and love, they become sleepwalkers, and worse, fanatics and zealots. Religion is both a gift and a problem. Organized, institutional religion, besides protecting its tradition and its original vision, often assumes authoritarian hierarchy, power and control. It becomes concerned primarily with survival and power. This part of religion does not want us to be become mature and free. It wants children who will faithfully obey, support and serve it. It alienates and is oppressive. Organized, institutional religion is necessary, it is good to belong to one, but one has to learn to keep one's critical distance and freedom.

Standing in the in-between of religions offers us today a most fruitful form of spirituality. One theologian talks of 'passing over' and coming back. Passing over, *pascha*, into another religious tradition and spirituality and then coming back to one's own, transformed and reformed. In passing over mind and heart into another one, one dies to one's own particular, self-enclosed religion; in coming back, one is born in spirit and truth. When we are identified totally with one religion, we lose our souls. Passing over and coming back, or better *standing in-between*, the spirit becomes freed and we come into our goodness and compassionate humanity. Standing in-between, the self stands nowhere and yet embraces all. The self is open to the infinite, yet its home is in the particular and the concrete, in the Here and the Now. It has no boundaries and no limits, yet it is through the door of the ethical life that it comes into life and reality.

Standing nowhere, let the mind come forth, challenges a *koan*. It urges you to realize ultimate reality and truth. No answer borrowed from others or from scriptures will do. You have to come to a personal Realization and actualization. It is a personal journey into a never ending horizon that is mystery. It is said that the saint will not know who she/he is until the consummation of the communion of the saints; which is to say, not until the end of time when all are gathered up. You cannot know your name apart from all the names of the world. Your Self is an openness to the All, which can be realized only in the journeying. The journey begins with the first step Here and Now. And every step is the first step. Where do you begin?

Meister Eckhart was asked, "Where does the soul go after death?" He replied, "Nowhere!" There is nowhere else than the Here and Now. There is a Sufi saying: "There is a time when you journey *towards* god and there is a time when you journey *in* god." Once you Awaken to reality, then all your life is nowhere else than in god. Perhaps not so much in god, as god herself living your life as 'I'.

Let me give you a Zen story:

A soldier named Nobushige came to Hakuin, and asked, "Is there really a paradise and a hell?" "Who are you?" inquired Hakuin. "I am a samurai," the warrior replied. "You, a soldier!" exclaimed Hakuin. "What kind of ruler would have you as his guard? Your face looks like that of a beggar." Nobushige became so angry that he began to draw his sword. But Hakuin continued, "So you have a sword! Your weapon is probably much too dull to cut off my head." As Nobushige drew his sword Hakuin remarked, "Here open the gates of hell!" At these words the samurai, perceiving the master's discipline, sheathed his sword and bowed. "Here open the gates of paradise," said Hakuin.

Our home is in the community of imperfect, wounded human beings. No relationship will be perfect and completely fulfilling; all relationships involve hurt and failures. This only calls us to learn to accept ourselves and let ourselves be accepted by others, in our neediness and imperfection. Courage and freedom arise in our standing in fidelity to this community of love. And they are nourished by gratitude and compassion. True religion and spirituality give us a vision of reality as mystery, mystery that is graciousness. You are held in love and you are love—learn how to love yourselves and to love all beings, *today*. To be love, in non-violence. Today is the day of salvation. "Today you will be in paradise with me," were the dying words of Jesus. Let me end with the beautiful and inspiring words of Rabbi Hillel:

If you are not friends with yourself,
Who will be?
If you are only that, what are you?
If not now, when?

Heart Broken, Heart of Love

Joshu went to a hermit's hut and asked, "Is the Master in? Is the Master in?" The hermit thrust up his fist. Joshu said, "The water is too shallow for a ship to anchor." Thereupon he left.

He went to another hermit's hut, and asked, "Is the Master in? Is the Master in?" The hermit thrust up his fist. Joshu said, "Freely you give, freely you take away. Freely you kill, freely you give life." He made a profound bow.

This event presumably took place during Joshu's pilgrimage after his master Nansen's death. Joshu is said to have vowed, "Even if he is a small child seven years old, if he is superior to me in any sense I will beg him to teach me. Even if he is an old man a hundred years old, if he is inferior to me I will teach him." Here he happens to visit two hermits and he tests them by challenging each to manifest the Master, or the True Self. The question, "Is the Master in?" could also be rendered as, "What is there?" Or, "Is there something here?" Or, "Do you have it?" It can also be rendered as, "Are you in?" Or, "Is anybody in?" In the Zen framework, Joshu's question is, "Is the true Self here?" Or, "Are you an Awakened one?" Or, "Show me your Awakened mind and heart."

Is the Master in? Have *you* realized It? *Where* do you stand? Have you come *Home*? *Who* are you? Well, each of the hermits answers in exactly the same way. "A fist is a fist throughout. Here is no room for discrimination," as Zen Master Shibayama comments. Yet, Joshu praises one and puts down other. What is the difference between them and their answers? Mumon, in his commentary on the *koan*, warns that you can neither say that there is a difference of superiority and inferiority between them, nor that there is no difference. How did Joshu judge and differentiate between them? Or can you say that he did not differentiate at all? If he did not differentiate, then was his tongue without bone, as Mumon comments? What was the mind of Joshu? Shibayama Roshi quotes a fine poem on this:

The spring breeze in a tree
Has two different faces:
A southward branch looks warm,
A northward branch looks cool.

Some might think that perhaps Joshu had some extraordinary insight into people. There is no indication of such paranormal ability here. Yamada Ko-Un Roshi suggests that Joshu was checking to see what sort of reaction the hermits had to the praise and to the blame. The *koan* can, of course, be used to see if one has gone beyond praise and blame; which is to say, if one has come to abide where there is no-abiding; if one has come to abide in the Self where differentiation is unity and unity is differentiation and where there is, at the same time, a going beyond all ideas of duality and unity. The hermit who is put down by Joshu, if he is an Enlightened one, would not in the least be bothered by the put-down, for everything is "empty", and there is no discrimination and duality. He is not supposed to be touched by sorrow or suffering.

But the danger is that all this becomes only an ego-trip, a 'god-trip', as Tibetan Buddhist Master Chogyam Trungpa would say. Buddhism divides the modes of existence into six realms: gods, jealous gods, human beings, animals, hungry ghosts and hell beings. Trungpa and many others would see these not as objective, independent realities or beings but as "the six complete worlds we create as the logical conclusions of such powerful emotional highlights as anger, greed, ignorance, lust, envy, and pride. Having disowned the power of our emotions and projected that power onto the world outside, we find ourselves trapped in a variety of ways and see no hope for escape." In Zen we talk about no-thought, Emptiness, oneness, clarity, transparency, openness, courage and joy. One is invited to let go all thinking and respond in terms of 'pure action'—just eating, just walking, just doing what you do unmoved by thoughts or emotions. Perfection, autonomy, independence, clear awareness become the hallmarks of the Enlightened life. All talk of living in the realm of Emptiness and openness, of the 'space-like nature' of the mind and 'clear light' is characteristic of the 'god realm'. It is, as Mumon warns, 'to wear chains with a yoke' or 'to be imprisoned inside two iron mountains'. True Awakening is, on the other hand, the Awakening of the broken heart. Let me tell you a modern story:

A father was teaching his little daughter to be less afraid and be more trusting and courageous by having her jump down the stairs. He put her on the second stair and said, "Jump, I will catch you." The little girl jumped and he caught her. He placed her on the third stair, she jumped and he caught her. On the fourth and the fifth and the sixth. Then the daughter jumped from the last and highest step, as before; the father stepped aside, the girl fell flat on her face. As she looked up, bleeding and crying, the father said, "Never trust a man, even if he is your own father."

Human life is filled with betrayals, abandonment, hurt, failure, humiliation, misunderstanding and disappointment. We are all in one way or another wounded beings. But we want to forget our vulnerability and brokenness, and we dream of going back to primal innocence and perfection. Zen, or any other spiritual path, can be used to feed such fantasy, and as an escape from life and the world. We begin life with a sense of primal trust; it is a sort of animal faith and innocence. Trust and faith in justice and goodness are ingrained in our hearts. But this faith and trust are self-centred and naïve, and in terms of *our* expectations and demands. We live in dreams of pure love, unalloyed goodness, total perfection, perfect sincerity and clarity. This world is one of my desires, my dreams, my hopes and my loves. This is the world of the Garden of Eden before the Fall. It is a narcissistic and self-enclosed world. We carry this notion of the ideal into the spiritual life too.

Let me quote the insightful psychologist James Hillman on betrayal: "What one longs for is not only to be contained in perfection by another who can never let one down. It goes beyond trust and betrayal by the other in a relationship. What one longs for is a situation where one is *protected from one's own* treachery and ambivalence, one's own Eve. In other words, primal trust in the paternal world means being in that Garden with god and all things *but* Eve."

"Love becomes possible *after* betrayal," says Hillman. Betrayal of oneself by oneself and betrayal by others, by close friends and beloved ones. One's heart has to be broken for true love to be born. Betrayal, abandonment, misunderstanding, failure, brokenness are the doors to the heart of love.

Betrayal is, above all, self-betrayal. In the first phase, as said earlier, we are each of us carried away by our own enthusiasm, idealism, romanticism; we are caught and carried away by our own emotions and fantasies. We see and experience the reality of the others and the world through our self-centred emotions and fantasies. Deluding ourselves that our emotions and imaginations are pure and selfless, we are unable to see the darker side. Thus we go on blithely blind to the reality and resistance of the other, blind to the otherness of the other. When reality breaks in, when our illusions are shattered, we feel abandoned, betrayed, broken. But we need to recognize that it is our hearts that have betrayed us— and that from such 'betrayal' and brokenness, love can be born.

Entry to true love is a matter of choice as well as of grace. The girl who has been betrayed by the father in the story "may be unable to forgive and so remain fixated in the trauma, revengeful, resentful, blind to any understanding and cut off from love." Or she can let her heart be opened up to unconditional love and compassion. First, Hillman mentions some of the 'sterile choices' she may make: revenge, denial, cynicism, paranoia and, above all, self-betrayal. Revenge only diminishes and devalues life. Primitive fantasies, bitterness, and desire for revenge can lock one for life, blighting life and love. Denial denies the value of the other person or denies and represses one's vulnerability, pain, humiliation and hurt. Cynicism can no more see values and ideals in oneself, others and the world—power and survival are the only values attributed to all of them. This can also lead to a paranoid stance. Paranoia "is a way of protecting oneself against ever being betrayed again". Self-betrayal is the worst of all. All of one's previous actions and words are suspect and seen as silly and ridiculous. "The alchemical process is reversed: the gold turned back into faeces, one's pearls cast before swine." One cannot trust one's own heart any more, one's values and love become suspect. One does not dare to live one's life at where one is and by one's vocation.

Zen talks about its prerequisites as Great Faith, Great Doubt and Great Questioning. Great Faith is, as the Korean Zen master Sung Bae Park explains, Patriarchal faith, which is the affirmation, "I am Buddha" rather than "I can become Buddha." Great Doubt is the doubt that negates this faith in the confession, "I am an ignorant sentient being." Great Questioning points to an unbroken process of inward questioning, which represents the dialectic struggle between the two poles of faith and doubt, or affirmation and negation. This is supposed to create an identity crisis that is resolved in Enlightenment—expressed in the Korean Sôn tradition as 'brokenness', *kkaech'im*. "What is broken in Enlightenment is one's dualistic intellectual framework and attachment to ego." Enlightenment as brokenness is very beautiful. However, such an Awakening or 'brokenness' is only the first step. The deepening and maturing of this 'brokenness' can only be realized in the in-between of human relationships. Great is primal faith and trust; but it is shattered and broken in betrayal and abandonment, in frustration and shame. This breakdown becomes the door to Great Trust and Unconditional Love. Such unconditional affirmation of the goodness of the world, life and others is true Awakening. Once again to quote Hillman, "Neither trust nor forgiveness would be fully realized without betrayal."

It is the motif of love and necessity that saves the betrayer from sadism and evil. For the betrayer, "Atonement also implies a submission to betrayal as such, its transpersonal fateful reality. By bowing before the shame of my inability to keep my word, I am forced to admit humbly both my own personal weakness and the reality of impersonal powers." The father has to bear in silence the sorrow and the pain. And the wrong has to be seen in a wider context than merely the personal or the psychological. And yet for reconciliation and 'soul-making' to be meaningful and transforming, the wrong and the suffering have to be recognized, remembered and held within the in-between of the human community and the betrayer and betrayed. The wronged one has to be recognized as an individual of dignity and worth. "The final integration of the experience may result in forgiveness by the betrayed, atonement by the betrayer, and a reconciliation—not necessarily with each other—but a reconciliation by each to the event. Each of these phases of bitterly fought and suffered experiences… may take long years of fidelity to the dark side of the psyche…"

In today's world we have been witnessing unspeakable horrors and evil—cruelty, betrayal, torture and rape, souls and bodies broken down under the unbearable burden of these. Such evil is individual as well as institutional and collective. If we can use such a word, it can be called absolute or radical evil. Is redemption possible through and beyond such evil and destruction? What we had been discussing earlier were the unavoidable complexities of human relationships and not about this 'absolute' evil. However, calling it 'absolute', or 'radical' may lead to the danger of giving substance and reality to evil, as if it were some reality equal to or standing over against the good.

Evil is basically *privatio boni*, privation of good—lack of what should have been there. According to Hannah Arendt, it is failure in being fully human. She called it the 'banality of evil', to point to evil as lack and shallowness, as a failure in true dialogue in community. Rene Girard points to evil as coming from mimetic desire, which is envy of the good held by the others and which leads to violence. Some see the fear and anxiety before one's mortality and extinction, which lead to grasping at power or immortality projects, as the root of evil. Others see the root of evil in human pride and self-assertion over and against human limits and the otherness of the others. If power is taken as the ultimate good of humans, which is the great temptation in today's world, it becomes evil. Often evil results from our choosing the partial or lesser good instead of the greater and the truer; from choosing power instead of the good; from loving the abstract—ideology, doctrine, collective commonality—instead of the concrete, finite existence and the individual person. All these can be seen as choosing one's self against—at the expense of—others or against the human condition itself.

Evil, however, as said earlier, is a deprivation, and not understandable in itself. Evil is real but is not some *thing* over and against the good, it has no independent existence; it is parasitic on the good. It is infection, deformation, distortion of human freedom and will. Evil is not an equal partner with good, evil and good are not 'two hands of god'. One cannot accept evil as such nor should one try to attack it directly. Beings as far as they *are*, are good. But there are consequences of evil deeds and actions, and there are victims and sufferers; they call us to action and compassion, not for explanations, reasons and causes, justifications, or theories. Compassion for ourselves and for the sufferers is the only answer. It involves turning your face steadily towards the good, the true, the beautiful. It means saying 'No' to evil, and choosing again and again the good and the true—not the in an abstract sense, but in concrete, living persons and beings.

In Zen, your primal faith and trust have to be broken through and transformed into Great Trust and Primordial Caring. Such transformation takes place through 'dying to oneself' and Awakening to Emptiness. This is made possible partly by entering into one's boundless space of consciousness and imagination. Transformation is to Awaken from negativity and denial to the Great Affirmation of life and world; a Great Amen, a Yes, which both transcends and includes your ordinary 'yes'es and 'no'es. It involves going through the night of suffering and darkness and, in and through them, reaching the Other Shore of the good, the true, the beautiful. Not even so much *reaching* the Other Shore as the Other Shore already flowing in, inhering and illumining this shore. The Transcendent, the Good, the True, the Beautiful flow in and illumine from the beyond, as well as embrace, redeem and transform the polarities of good and bad, darkness and light, birth and death. Then each and every being and person is seen in his or her suchness, as gift and grace; each is the face of Emptiness that is Mystery. Each being and each event is the call of the Self to the Self.

Now tell me, how will you answer the call of Joshu the Terrible: is the Self in? Are *you* in? *Who* is that who is calling? *Who* is answering? When you have been hurt: is the Self in? When you have been betrayed, or when you have failed: is the Self in? *From where* do you come? What is the space you stand in? And what do you *see*? True seeing is Emptiness seeing Emptiness.

When confronted with suffering and evil, how do you see? How do you hear?

The Way of the Heart-Mind

> *Joshu addressed the assembly: "The real Way is not difficult. It only abhors choice and attachment. With but a single word there may arise choice and attachment or there may arise clarity. Do you appreciate the meaning of this or not?"*
>
> *A monk asked, "If you do not have that clarity, what do you appreciate?"*
>
> *Joshu said, "I do not know that, either."*
>
> *The monk said, "If you do not know, how can you say you do not have that clarity?"*
>
> *Joshu said, "Asking the question is good enough. Now make your bows and retire."*

'The real Way is not difficult' is the first line of an ancient Zen poem, *On Believing in the Mind.* The real or ultimate Way is a translation of 'Tao'. Tao meant 'a way or passage where people come and go'. Tao is the all-embracing first principle from which all the universe and all that *is* arise. It is nameless and unnamable. All things come from Tao and return to Tao. Yet it also meant the practical as well as the right way of human living and behaviour. In Zen, attaining Tao is attaining Awakening.

In this encounter, Joshu says that as soon as words are spoken, there is a 'getting attached to': we get attached to either picking and choosing or to clarity which is Emptiness.

He also makes the point that discrimination and choice are not in themselves the problem. The problem lies in our identifying one thing or another—desires, experiences, ideas, persons or whatever—as one's self, and as ultimate security and ground. "Tao does not belong to knowing or to not-knowing," Nansen tells Joshu. And thus, "Ordinary Mind is the Tao."

But what about our daily life of discrimination and choices? Even to decide to let-go deciding is a decision. Can we ever escape thought, judgement, decision and the consequent action? To live is to discriminate and decide. So the monk is challenging Joshu: you say you don't abide anywhere or do not have that discriminating clarity— how do you *know* that then? Even to know that you do not know is knowing and clarity! Joshu tells the monk, you have asked enough; now make your bows and withdraw. Cornered and unable to answer, is Joshu taking refuge in his authority? Where is Joshu here?

To attain Awakening is to Awaken to Emptiness; it is to realize the world-as-the-self and the self-as-the-world. "From the standpoint of the world, I-myself am the world. From the standpoint of I-myself, the world is I-myself. When the world is I-myself, there is no self. When there is no self, the whole world is nothing but I-myself, and this is the true no-mind in Zen. When one lives with this no-mind, can there be anything to obstruct I-myself? What can there be, then, to restrict the world?" comments Shibayama Roshi.

Awakening is finding one's subject Self as no other than the Tao, the ultimate Subject. Then all the world is the coming forth of the One Self.

> *Unmon held out his staff and said to the assembled monks, "The staff has transformed itself into a dragon and swallowed up the universe! Where are the mountains, the rivers, and the great world?*

The staff is the One Self. The entire world is but the revelation of this One Self. Engo in his introduction to this *koan* says, "Mountains, rivers, and your own self are all just the same. Why should they be separate and constitute two worlds? Even if you are well versed in Zen *koans* and know how to deal with them, if you stop there everything is spoiled." Where then can you stop or stand? If the whole universe is your self, where do you stand and where do you go? Joshu's simple answer is, "I don't know." Emperor Wu of Liang asked Bodhidharma, "Who are you standing before me?" Bodhidharma replied, "I don't know." 'I don't know', however, is not enough. *Standing nowhere, let the mind come forth* runs a *koan*—how do you do that? Joshu answers, "Asking the question is enough, now make your bows and retire." Joshu is *showing* the Great Way. Do you see that? Part of Setcho's verse to the *koan* sings:

> *Far away in the heavens the sun rises, the moon sets;*
> *Beyond the hills the high mountains, the cold waters.*
> *The skull has no consciousness, no delight;*
> *The dead tree sings in the wind, not yet rotten.*

"Heaven and earth spring from the same root as myself, and all things are one with me": these words are from *Chao Luen* of Seng-chao, written in the late fourth century; Shih-t'ou came to Awakening reading this treatise. When Shih-t'ou came to the sentence, "Who but the Sage can realize that all things are one with himself?" he exclaimed, "The Sage is selfless, and therefore to him there is nothing that is not himself. The *Dharmakaya* is formless, where can the distinction between the Self and the Other come in? ...As there is no duality between the knowing and the known, how can there be any talk of going and coming? Oh, what a supreme vision is unfolded by those words!"

But the danger here is that you may get stuck with these beautiful words—"if you stop there everything is spoiled." Hence, Master Nansen cuts short Riku Taifu who quotes admiringly these words of Seng-chao. Engo in his verse to this *koan* again warns, "Mountains and rivers should not be viewed in the mirror." Will paper cake satisfy your hunger? When Unmon was asked, "What is Tao?" he uttered just one word, "Go!" which can also be translated as "Walk on!"

Awakening to the Tao flows into *willingness* as against *willfulness*, as authors Kurtz and Ketcham phrase it. Willingness is saying 'yes' to oneself and others, to world and life. It is in a way similar to what Dag Hammarskjoeld writes in his diary for Whitsunday, 1961: "I don't know who—or what—put the question, I don't know when it was put. I don't even remember answering. But at some moment I did answer *Yes* to Someone—or Something—and from that hour I was certain that existence is meaningful and that, therefore, my life, in self-surrender, had a goal. From that moment I have known what it means 'not to look back', and 'to take no thought for the morrow.'"

Willfulness is the attempt to manipulate and control others and oneself. Objects can be controlled, problems can be solved. But persons are 'ends' in themselves as opposed to objects, they are 'mystery' as opposed to problems. Similariy, there are certain pursuits that we can will ourselves into, whereas the states of mind they induce cannot be willed. For example, knowledge can be directly willed but not wisdom; so also pleasure versus happiness, congratulations versus admiration, reading/listening versus understanding, etc. To will what cannot be willed is to become 'addicted to addiction'. It is also the difference between magic and miracle. "Miracle involves openness to mystery, the welcoming of surprise, the acceptance of those realities over which we have no control. Magic is the attempt to be in control, to manage everything—it is the claim to be, or to have a special relationship with, some kind of 'god'."

Willfulness manifests in our unwillingness to be patient with ourselves, to respect the otherness of the others, to accept our imperfect lives, to let ourselves be changed in the course of time; to accept the human condition of finitude, mortality, vulnerability, imperfection, interdependence as well as the uncertainty, ambiguity and paradox of life and reality. It is the symptom and illusion of our being identified with our ego-self and is the 'disorder of will'.

When you Awaken to the realization of your Self as no other than the Tao, what are you greedy for? And what are you running to or running away from? But if you appropriate this realization to your ego-self, then it is only ego inflation and sterile narcissism. The ego-self's true life is to be openness to the Self. In this openness each and everything comes as a miracle and revelation; the other person is other to you and yet not-other and that is grace and gift.

Taoism has touched Zen deeply and thus Tao appears naturally in this *mondo* or *koan*. The Taoist ideal of *wu-wei*, the spontaneous action in non-action, colours Joshu's answers in this *mondo* and exemplifies what has been said about willingness. *Wu-wei* literally means 'in the absence of/without doing' and was later translated as 'non-action'. It is not so much behaviour as a state of mind of the actor. In his book, *Effortless Action: The Chinese Spiritual Ideal of Wu-wei*, Slingerland says of *wu-wei*, "It describes a state of personal harmony in which actions flow freely and instantly from one's spontaneous inclinations—without the need for extended deliberation or inner struggle—and yet nonetheless perfectly accord with the dictates of the situation at hand..."

Wu-wei cannot be turned into a means to something else or made into an object of pursuit. It is not simply a lifestyle, not a mere subjective way of being and doing. It is the embodied mind of humans conforming to the Way of Heaven. Only by embodying the Way in all of one's actions does one become the fully realized human being. Thus Heaven, the Way, *wu-wei*, and virtue are intimately linked with one another. The embodied mind in accord with the Way is manifested in "spontaneous action that flows forth from the individual with no sense of effort and yet accords perfectly with the dictates of the situation and yields wonderful results... this ideal state [is] attainable only through a complete rejection and negation of all conventional values and conceptions of action."

Is Tao innate in humans or is one to learn and acquire it? This is an apparently tricky question. If innate in humans, why do humans not act accordingly? Why then is there so much evil and disorder among us? Zen struggles with it too. If it is not innate and has to be learned and acquired, how can one be moved to it? Ordinary craft or skill can be learned; but virtue and ethics can be actualized only when one is in the right state of mind and character. Aristotle says, "If we do what is just or temperate, we must already be just or temperate." He also says, "To become just we must first do just actions."

Like *wu-wei*, "..the paradox of virtue revolves around the fact that virtue can only be acquired by someone who is not consciously trying to acquire it. That is, performing a virtuous act while at the same time being self-conscious of its virtuousness makes it, paradoxically, not fully virtuous."

Even the great Master Joshu cannot solve the problem for the monk. It is not a problem to be solved; it is mystery one is called to live with. He is called to answer and he answers to the question, by way of *solvitur ambulando*, as the Latin phrase puts it, by 'walking' with the other, so to say, and thus bearing witness to the Tao, the Great Way.

All that has been said so far can be better caught in the symbol of the heart: the Way is the way of the heart. The heart is a multivalent and multilayered symbol; it denotes the centre of the whole person, it is the root and source of cognition, affection, consciousness, imagination and freedom; it is openness within and without, and yet its depths are hidden and mysterious. "The heart has reasons which reason does not know." Realization is Awakening to the identity of one's heart-mind with the heart-mind of heaven and earth, with that 'love that moves the sun and the stars'. The Way is to embody the heart-mind of heaven and earth as one's own heart-mind. The 12th century mystic Chu Hsi made this impassioned cry: "The heart-mind of the ten thousand things is like the heart-mind of heaven and earth. The heart-mind of all under heaven is like the heart-mind of the sages. With heaven and earth's giving life to the ten thousand things, there is a heart-mind of heaven and earth in each thing. With the sages in the world, every person has a heart-mind of the sages." Or again: "Heaven and earth generalize and extends its heart-mind to the ten thousand things. Human beings obtain this and bring it to completion as the human heart-mind. Things obtain this and bring it to completion as the heart-mind of things. Grass and trees, birds and beasts receive it, and set it forth to completion as the heart-mind of grass and trees, birds and beasts. These are nothing but the heart-mind of heaven and earth."

This heart-mind of heaven and earth is manifested in humans above all as the heart-mind's capacity for spiritual efficacy and creative functioning. The human heart-mind is, in other words, the openness to heaven and earth; not only mere openness—it is the dwelling place of heaven and earth as well as their creative functioning. The human other in particular is the concrete embodiment of heaven and earth and the Awakened heart-mind is made captive to this other, whereby love and truth become one. It is thus that Emptiness is realized and actualized.

Here is a *mondo* expressing the heart-mind of Joshu:

> Someone asked, *"You are such a saintly personality. Where would you find yourself after your death?"*
> Joshu replied, *"I go to hell ahead of you all!"*
> The questioner was thunderstruck and said, *"How could that be?"*
>
> The master did not hesitate. *"Without my first going to hell, who would be waiting there to save people like you?"*

Another similar one:

> *Joshu was approached by an old lady who said, "Women are considered to be heavily laden with the five obstructions. How can I be freed from them?" The master said, "Let all the other people be born in Heaven but may I this old woman be forever drowned in the ocean of suffering."*

Masao Abe comments: "(Joshu's) seemingly harsh reply springs from great compassion in which no distinction between Joshu and the old woman exists and in which Joshu himself is willing to suffer much more than or in place of anyone else. I understand it was to emphasize this point that, identifying Joshu with the old woman, Suzuki translated this portion as 'May *I this* old woman be forever drowned in the ocean of suffering.' " It is the same heart-mind of Joshu manifesting itself in the following *mondo* as well:

> *A monk asked Joshu in all earnestness, "What is the meaning of the patriarch coming from the West?" Joshu said, "The oak tree in the front of the garden."*

The realization of the identity of your heart-mind with the heart-mind of heaven and earth involves a *conversion* of heart and *transformation*, or as T S Eliot puts it, "purification of our desires in the ground of beseeching." Chu Hsi states, "When a scholar disciplines himself in overcoming the ego and returning to propriety to the point of eliminating egocentric desires completely, then his [heart-]mind is purely this [heart-]mind of Heaven and Earth giving life to things."

In the words of Pierre-François de Bethune: "But whatever the path, the stages of Zen will be those of maturation of the 'heart': *mu-shin*, the heart despoiled, should become unified heart, *i-shin*, and an Awakened heart, *myo-shin*. For the goal of this journey is always *hei-jo-shin*, the daily heart, that is to say, a behaviour that responds simply to the needs of the moment, but in a coherent way, truly free."

How to transcend or go beyond all the contradictions and oppositions of life and reality? How do you realize the way beyond words and non-words, subjectivity and objectivity? What is the Way?

> *A monk once asked Master Fuketsu, "Both speaking and silence are concerned with relativity. How can we be free and non-transgressing?" Fuketsu said,*
>
> *"How fondly I remember Konan in March! The partridges are calling, and the flowers are fragrant."*

Everyday Mind is the Way

Joshu asked Nansen, "What is the Way?" Nansen replied, "The ordinary mind is the Way." Joshu asked, "Should I direct myself towards it or not?" Nansen said, "If you try to turn towards it, you go against it." Joshu asked, "If I do not try to turn towards it, how can I know that it is the Way?"

Nansen answered, "The Way does not belong to knowing or not-knowing. Knowing is delusion, not-knowing is blank consciousness. When you have reached the true Way beyond all doubt, you will find it as vast and boundless as outer space. How can it be talked about on a level of right and wrong?" At these words, Joshu was suddenly Enlightened.

Joshu came to Master Nansen in his teens and had his first taste of Enlightenment when he was 18 years old. In true Zen tradition, he still had to deepen and purify his Realization and he spent the next 40 years or so training under his master. After Nansen's death, he spent about 20 years as a fiercely independent wandering monk, quick to dismiss charlatans but ever ready to learn from Enlightened masters. It was only after this that he finally settled down to teach and came to be known as a very great master, 'the old Buddha'. This particular encounter that I have quoted is believed to have taken place during the early phase of his training under Nansen, some time after his initial glimpse of Enlightenment.

Zen follows the Mahayana dictum, *samsara is Nirvana and Nirvana is samsara*. *Samsara*, we all know, is our ordinary life of birth and death. What of Nirvana? We get ourselves caught up in many ideas about Nirvana—the ultimate Enlightenment, nothingness, state of godhood and so on.

This is the Zen pointer to Nirvana: this very life of ours is the life of Nirvana! *Samsara is Nirvana and Nirvana is samsara.* And so it is that Layman Pang exclaims after his Enlightenment:

> *Wondrous power,*
> *Marvellous activity:*
> *I draw water,*
> *Split firewood!*

And the great Hakuin sings:

> *Nirvana is right here before our eyes;*
> *This very place is the Lotus Land,*
> *This very body the Buddha.*

Your very life, this very world, and each and every thing in it, is a miracle and a wonder. Hakuin scolds you, the seeker of Nirvana outside of your very life, in this impassioned cry: "You are like a person standing in the midst of water and crying out in thirst!"

> *Master Kempo was asked, "Where is the way to Nirvana?" He lifted his stick, drew a line, and said, "Here it is." A monk once asked his master about Kempo's One Way and how to enter it. The master asked him, "Do you hear the stream running? (There was a stream running nearby.) Well, enter there!" The monk then asked, "Suppose there was no stream and no sound?" The master called the*

monk by name; the monk immediately responded, "Yes!" The master said, "Enter there!"

Everyday heart-mind is the heart-mind of the Buddha. As we recite in the Ten Verse Kannon *Sutra*,

Thought after thought arises in the heart-mind,
Thought after thought is not separate from the Heart-Mind.

Your heart-mind is not other than the heart-mind of the Buddha. But it is covered with delusion and ignorance, greed and hatred. It is our Zen task to Awaken to the selfless heart-mind, to the Formless Self that is Emptiness. To the question "What is Buddha?" Basho answered, "This very mind is Buddha." Asked the same question another time he said, "No mind, no Buddha." The Diamond Sutra cryptically declares: "The world is not the world, therefore the world is the world." Mahayana Buddhism speaks of the *bodhicitta*, the heart-mind of Awakening for self and all beings.

But to enter this very mind of the Buddha, we have to die and be reborn. Only then can we say that we have come to the Buddha-mind, Buddha-heart. This dying is to let go all attachments and self-definitions, and to surrender into the abyss that is Emptiness that is graciousness. It is to realize, in the words of Tung-shan, "He is the same as you, but you are not the same as He." You are not apart from ultimate reality; ultimate reality is your very Self. Enlightenment is to Awaken to the world as the Self and the Self as the world. It is the Realization of your Self as but an openness, openness to the all. At the same time, it is acceptance and affirmation of your finite self and finite life. It brings about a trust and faith that can be called unconditional. Whose trust is it? Who trusts whom?

With no hindrance in the mind;
No hindrance, thus no fear

says the Heart Sutra.

Without such Awakening and Realization, everyday mind is only the deluded mind and deluded heart. Human beings are beings of desires and longing. Our hearts are filled with the desires of the world and our own deepest desires are often unknown. And there is in each of us a unique call, a vocation/call itself is vocation driving us ceaselessly. There are desires that can be fulfilled and desires that cannot be fulfilled.

The desire for the Beyond, the Invisible, the Unknowable, the Infinite is not so much our desire as the desire of the cosmos, or of the Buddha, or of the Spirit. It calls us to hope in the midst of hopelessness, love in midst of hatred and evil, trust where no ground for trust is visible, step out of our conceptual boundaries and bondage. It is a desire that can be fulfilled only in the heart of faith and love where all things are possible. It is this desire that declares itself in the Four Great Vows of the bodhisattva: 'Though the Way of the Awakened is unsurpassed, I vow to walk along all the Way.'

> *Bodhidharma, the First Patriarch of Zen, sat facing the wall. His chief disciple, who was later to become the Second Patriarch, stood in the snow, cut off his arm and said, "Your disciple's mind is not yet at peace. I beg you, master, give it rest." Bodhidharma said, "Bring your mind to me and I will put it to rest." The Patriarch replied, "I have searched for the mind but have never been able to find it." Bodhidharma said, "I have thoroughly set it at rest for you."*

The heart and mind have come to a peace that the world cannot give. But desires still well up, and the flowers bloom and fall. Besides, the desire for the Beyond is only deepened. It has now become the call of our unique vocation. It is by living by our vocation that we find meaning in life. We are not meant to be well-balanced, sober servants of the collective values; we are meant to be unique and different. I quote Jung: "What is it, in the end, that induces a man to go his own way and to rise out of unconscious identity with the mass as out of a swathing mist? ...It is what is commonly called vocation: an irrational factor that destines a man to emancipate himself from the herd and from its well-worn paths. True personality is always a vocation and puts its trust in it as in god... Anyone with a vocation hears the voice of the inner man: he is *called.*" The shape and character of our vocation will change at different development stages. Personality or personhood is not found in adjusting to external expectations but in serving one's calling in the context of our environment. Something in us, no matter how much we flee it, summons us. We may avoid it all our lives, but deep down, something knows. It knows us whether we wish to know it or not.

Awakening to Emptiness has to flow into a commitment to your concrete vocation and life. Awakening, of course, is Awakening to Emptiness and oneness, or better, non-duality of self and world. But merely to stay there is to live in the 'Zen hole'. That would be just an ego trip, the stink of Zen. You are Buddha-self, you live in Buddha-nature. But this is of no use unless you actualize your Buddha-self and Buddha-nature in the world in terms of truthfulness, goodness, justice, mercy and love. We have to, in a way of speaking, descend from the realm of the gods, from that of the deathless and formless, the universal and the abstract openness into that of the concrete singular, particular, personal and mortal. We have to embrace the concrete universal, so to say, and consent to our own death. "*Where is your birth in karma?*" asks a *koan*. Karma here means the world of space and time, cause and effect.

We have to commit ourselves to values in our relationship to others. We have to take responsibility for ourselves, for our relationships and for the world. It means freely entering into dialogue with others as well as with oneself; it involves learning to listen, understand, judge, choose and act. It calls for promise and fidelity to others. It may involve making mistakes and failures, hurting and getting hurt. This is the human condition. "An Enlightened monk falls into a well!" We are 'shitting angels' — sometimes all shitting, sometimes all angelic! There is a danger in spiritually inclined people, that they expect that spirituality and meditation will free them from such human involvements and responsibility; that life will become miraculously spontaneous and free, without the painful need to listen, understand, judge and choose; that they can achieve pure action, action with no thought and no reflection; that they can dwell in the god realm, and be angelic all the time. Save yourself from such delusions. Renounce the search for magical powers, keep the flame of passion for the impossible burning and at the same time learn to practise the art of the possible Here and Now.

There is an old Zen story that goes like this: once there lived an old woman who had supported a monk for over twenty years——she had housed him in a hut and fed him while he was absorbed in spiritual practice. Came the day she decided to check the adept's progress. She hired a girl to go to the monk, embrace him and ask him what he was going to do about it. The girl did as instructed, and when she embraced him, the monk said to her, "An old tree grows on a cold rock in winter. Nowhere is there any warmth." The girl reported her experience to the old woman. The old woman was furious. "To think I fed the fellow for twenty years," she raged. "He showed no consideration for your need, no disposition to explain your condition. He need not have responded to your passion, but he could have at least shown some compassion." She went to the monk's hut and burned it down.

The monk has suppressed his emotions and become attached to his detachment from passions. Without passions, there can be no compassion. He is self-enclosed and is not able to pay attention to 'the other who comes' and respond.

Emotions and passions are what make us human. Without these, we cannot even think and decide, we might as well be dead persons walking. Emotions and passions are our heart and soul. There is a danger in Zen that one tries to suppress all emotions for fear of attachment and commitment. Or to go to the other extreme and indulge one's passions with the justification of the Zen saying, 'passions are *bodhi*'. Passions are *bodhi*, but that is only half the truth. Emotions become meaningful only in commitment to values in terms of others and the world. Emotions and imagination overflow our bounded selves and break us open to the world and others. They are not simply ours, we do not just own them. Emotions are the call and address of the others to us—not the general others, but the particular, concrete, individual persons. We have to let the other be other, respect and accept the strangeness and otherness of the other person, though it can be frightening and dangerous to our ego-self.

It is the plight of our human condition that we allow our emotions and passions to become distorted and perverted. It is not even enough to come to Enlightenment; one has to learn how to cultivate and be sensitive to emotions in service of the ethical and the true, the good and the just. Only such commitment gives one actual freedom. I'll be the first to admit that many an 'Enlightened' Zen master has been guilty of the most atrocious conduct. Stories of abuse of power at Zen centres and monasteries are legion. During World War II many Zen masters and monks in Japan inflamed passions, blinded by prejudice and nationalist jingoism.

What went wrong with their Zen and Enlightenment? Their Awakening was not the Awakening of the heart-mind converted. They forgot to deal with the question of power in living. The Enlightened one has to learn how to cultivate and exercise power in service of goodness and justice. Not only the Enlightened but all of us need to learn to handle our power and authority. Actually, emotions and passions are energy and we have to learn to channel the energy rightly. Do not be ruled and controlled by the energy, do not repress and deny the energy. Your life and existence are energy, movement and power; know how to move and act, how to discern the true from the false, how to say 'no' and how to say 'yes'. This is the power of the sharp sword of *prajna* and *karuna*, wisdom and compassion. To ignore the question of power will lead only to demonic Zen. Everyday Zen is practice in the discernment and exercise of passions, emotions, and power in relationships and life in the world.

Let me tell you a story: a monk was crossing a river in a boat with some young men. The monk soon closed his eyes and was in *samadhi*. The young men, seeing the holy monk in meditation, could not resist subjecting him to their irreverence and ridicule. They began throwing banana peels at the monk, joking that the holy one was no more than a discarded banana peel. Suddenly, a voice was heard from nowhere: "Son, your enemies are persecuting you; if you so wish, I will overturn the boat and destroy all of them." The matter looked serious, for the young ones were not without some superstition, and everyone became quiet, wondering what the monk was going to do. The monk opened his eyes, looked around, and said, "God, you are speaking like Satan: why do you want to overturn the boat and destroy all of them? If you like, do overturn and convert their hearts and minds." After a short silence, a voice was once more heard, "My son, the voice you heard first was not my voice but that of Satan!"

Not all inspirations, not all spirits are good and life giving. To live is to discern and choose, to change and move, to respond and act in *dialogue with others*. Such a life is filled with ambiguities and uncertainties, risks and failures. Life is full of complexity and multiplicity, darkness, evil and meaninglessness, chaos and absurdities. There is no absolute guarantee and security for our choices and vision. There is in humans a great anxiety in the face of such finitude and absurdity. Faced with this, the 'everydayness' of many of us is often a mask that hides cowardice and fear.

To Awaken is to fall into this abyss and come alive to the goodness and the grace-filled nature of life, even as we recognize that there is no absolute security. We need to come to such a vision of life and reality and, we also need the faith and courage to affirm our vision by our decisions and actions. We need to be unfettered by established conventions and mores, beliefs and systems. Yet we need to affirm life and be attentive to the needs of community, of self and others. In short, we have to bear witness to faith, trust and love by our compassionate caring and way of living.

Isan and his disciple Kyozan were the co-founders of the Igyo School of Zen in China. One day Isan asked Kyozan, "How many years has it been since you completely rid yourself of even the finest traces of delusion?" 'Finest traces of delusion' refers to delusions that remain even after we have attained Enlightenment and have practised for many years. Kyozan asked in return, "How about you, Master?" Isan replied, "It has been seven years since I entered this mountain and completely rid myself of even the finest traces of delusion." Isan repeated his question to Kyozan. Kyozan answered, "Me, Master? I am busy from morning to night without a moment's rest!"

It is the same Isan who when asked where he would go after death replied that he would go down to the village and become a buffalo there!

Awakened, everyday life is a life of joy. There is the joy of being; there is the joy of being alive, of living in the Here and Now, responding to life in the movement and action of all of our senses and abilities; there is the joy of excellence and achievement. The joy I refer to here is not simply sensual or physiological joy. This joy is the joy of just being and it is a gift. There can be joy in the midst of suffering and sorrows. In one sense our joy is not apart from sorrow.

The great Master Basho was seriously ill. The chief priest of the temple came to pay his respects. He asked, "How do you feel these days?" The Master said, "Sun-face Buddha, Moon-face Buddha."

Even in his deathbed, Basho is teaching us compassion; he is *presenting* the Buddha-self. The terms Sun-face Buddha and Moon-face Buddha are names of Buddhas, one living for one day only, the other for endless time; here they are taken to refer to Basho's changing health condition from day to day, moment to moment— 'Now I am short of breath and now I am not so bad.' *There is no other Buddha than this one here.* But to stop just with that is to short-change the light of Basho's face. In reality, Master Basho's life is lived 'in the face of' the Buddha as well 'being the face' of the Buddha. Only when you realize this do you 'see face to face with Buddhas and Patriarchs and walk hand in hand with them'. This is exemplified in the way of *dokusan*, the face-to-face encounter with the master in the private room. You enter the presence of the master and present your understanding and Realization, *as though* the master was not there: 'I alone between heaven and earth'. This 'I alone' is the Formless

Self and yet it is actualized only 'in the presence of' the Formless Self of the master. This living 'in the presence of' Emptiness that is the Formless Self as well as living as the Formless Self comes to manifestation in the 'face' of each person and thing in the world. Each is the 'face' of Emptiness that is Mystery; each is your very self appearing 'before' you and addressing you. It is mutual address and affirmation—you are affirmed by the call of the cuckoo and the cuckoo is affirmed by you. It is the joy of mutual knowing and recognition and sorrow.

> *The master of Rengeho cottage held out his staff and said to his disciples, "When, in olden times, a man reached the state of Enlightenment, why did he not remain there?"*
>
> *No one could answer, and he replied for them, "Because it is of no use in the course of life."*
>
> *And again he asked, "After all, what will you do with it?" And once again he said in their stead, "Taking no notice of others,*
> *Throwing his staff over his shoulder,*
> *He goes straight ahead and journeys*
> *Deep into the recesses of the hundred thousand mountains."*

Why did the Enlightened ones not stay there? Because attachment to Emptiness is the devil's stinking hole. 'Recesses of hundred thousand mountains' here refers to life's delusions and passions. The Enlightened one enters the marketplace with empty hands.

'Throwing his staff over his shoulders': what is that staff? 'Throwing the staff over the shoulders and journeying': how do you do that?

Awakening

For many years I dug the earth and searched for the blue heaven,
And how often, how often did my heart grow heavier and heavier.
One night, in the dark, I took stone and brick,
And mindlessly struck the bones of the empty heavens.

— Muso (14th century)

Taking hold, one's astray in nothingness;
Letting go, the Origin's regained.
Since the music stopped, no shadow's touched
My door: again the village moon's above the river.

— Kokai (15th century) of the Rinzai school

Why, it's but the motion of eyes and brow!
And here I've been seeking it far wide.
Awakened at last, I find the moon
Above the pines, the river surging high.

— Yuishan (16th century) of the Soto school

"In that instant, he attained Enlightenment."

This is how most *koan* stories end. It is a pivotal moment in the Zen tradition, the very essence, you could say, of Zen. What is this Enlightenment, this Great Awakening, that comes in a sudden, explosive instant as satori, or silently, in the deep repose of samadhi, as luminous prajna or Great Wisdom?

Say one word, admonishes Zen, and all is lost. For "the Way is beyond language." Yet this Awakening must be communicated, must be shared "with all sentient beings". The Ch'an masters of ancient times used paradox and quixotic action, and the Japanese masters of later times used the metaphor and symbolism of poetry to utter the 'unutterable'.

"That is it, that is it," Zen Master Yamada Ko-Un exclaimed when AMA Samy came to Awakening with the *koan*, *Who am I?* But it was, as AMA Samy saw it, only the beginning, the 'initial glimpse'. In his own words:

"There is a *koan* that goes, 'Where do you go after death?' I struggled for a long time with this *koan*. When I 'passed' it with Yamada Roshi, I was very excited. Then I forgot all about it. But it came back to me. When I reached my middle age, this *koan* came back again and again, asking, what is the self, what survives after death. I had already passed many *koans* and had had many 'experiences', yet I struggled again, for years and years, with this, my life *koan*, until I came to a deep Realization."

This section is a lucid and rare articulation of the dynamics of Zen Awakening. It has been put together from the early writings of Master AMA Samy. "Realize you are Emptiness," he ceaselessly tells his students. And always adds: "The Realization is incomplete unless you manifest this Emptiness that is your True Self in your *everyday life*." Zen Realization, in other words, is incomplete without Zen action.

Deeply rooted in the transcendental wisdom of the Upanishads, the loving compassion of the Christ, the profound thusness of Zen Realization, yet standing in the 'in-between of religions', Master AMA Samy brings a fresh—and uncompromising—perspective to the Awakened, Enlightened life. Not stopping with the Zen shout of Awakening, but manifesting it in the response to the call of life, to issue forth from the Emptiness to a life lived in joy and compassion.

Editor

Mountains are not Mountains, Rivers are not Rivers

One day when I was in Chennai, I went for a walk on the beach. My mind and heart were filled with trouble and pain. I could not get along with my superior, some of my students were creating problems, my Zen 'home-base' in Japan was undergoing a crisis, my financial situation was not good. After some time, I lifted my head and looked into the distance. My eyes fell on the waving palm trees, a church spire rising in their midst. In a flash, there was a deep, ineffable peace and equanimity in my heart. The problems had lost their force. My feelings could be expressed in the Zen saying of Unmon: "Everyday is a good day." Or, in the words of Julian of Norwich, "All shall be well, all manner of things shall be well." The sun was setting, the whole sky was lit in beauty. Tears welled in my eyes, tears of peace and equanimity.

Set against the context of my whole life this is a small event, an insignificant moment. But our ordinary lives are made up of such minor, small incidents and events and we have to pay attention to each and every one of them.

In our daily lives, there may be many such moments of simple awareness and just-being. They are moments of great repose and calm when the self is completely non-attached and dwells in a state of just-being, at peace with itself and the rest of the world. It is this state that basic Zen practice leads us to.

It is tempting to assume that there is no greater Reality than the just-being of such moments. But we need to go beyond. We need to penetrate deeply into the experience of just-being to enter the dimension of beyond-just-being.

As you deepen your Zen practice, you enter this dimension of beyond-just-being, Emptiness. But even that is not enough. There is a further step, which is the revelation that comes as an 'overturning of the base'; a world-shattering moment when the old order passes away and a new world is born. From the dimension of beyond-just-being we re-enter the dimension of just-being. It is in that instant of re-entry, in that instant of 'becoming', that our Original Face is revealed to us, in a grand symphony of being and becoming, Emptiness and manifestation, voidness and creation, all 'happening' in the same instant. Emptiness manifests and thereby becomes conscious of Itself. This is *prajna*, the Great Wisdom that comes as a sudden insight, that Zen practice can reveal to us.

In Zen practice, we surrender ourselves again and again to the beyond-just-being dimension that is Emptiness. Our daily life is then rooted in and flows from this new ground. We use terms like new world and new ground. But there is nothing new out there. What is happening is that the way we see our old world has undergone a radical transformation. Because we are now able to see it from the ground that is no-ground. Our seeing is now a Zen seeing. Our heart-mind is Awakened to Emptiness that is Mystery; it abides in darkness and unknowing, in faith and trust, where darkness itself is light.

Jizo asked Hogen, "Where are you going?"
Hogen said, "I am wandering at random."
Jizo said, "What do you think of wandering?"

Hogen said, "I do not know."
Jizo said, "Not-knowing is most intimate."
Hogen was suddenly Awakened.

When Bodhidharma was asked by the Emperor Wu of Liang what the ultimate, holy truth is, he answered, "Emptiness, no holiness." To the further question, "Who is it who is standing before me?" Bodhidharma replied, "I don't know."

'I don't know', 'not-knowing', is most intimate; this is your very Self, which cannot be captured in words and concepts. It is beyond discrimination, analysis, explanation and reasoning. It is beyond subject and object. Can you ever grasp the Self? Ask yourself the question: 'Who am I?' Whatever answer you give, is there not always the further question: Who is it that answers? Can you then ever know the Self? It is like the horizon, which recedes farther away the further you move towards it. So the 'knowing' in Zen is really a 'not-knowing'. At the same time it is your most intimate heart-mind. It is I myself and more than myself. Let's explore this in greater detail.

This not-knowing, Emptiness dimension in us is the openness to all; it is the dimension of be-ing, of is-ness, AM. We have to learn more and more to be rooted in this dimension. We should learn to come forth into the activities of our lives from this dimension. It is both our being and a call to us. In this Emptiness that is infinite openness of the Self, we are called to let go and surrender ourselves to the Now, to our openness and *isness*.

Zen meditation leads us to this *isness* that is Awakening. How is this offered to us? Does it come to us as a sudden blinding flash of light, as a great feeling of bliss, as a sudden ecstasy, in short, as some sort of experience? Is it an 'experience' that we come to in *zazen*?

There is a problem with the word 'experience', because it lends itself easily to misuse. People tend to hanker after experiences in meditation, the more psychedelic the better. 'Having an experience' is no big deal; a hard thump on the head, a dose of drugs, asphyxiation or deprivation of oxygen, auto-suggestion or hypnosis can give you great 'experiences'. Sometimes, people talk glibly of having had 'an experience of Emptiness'. But the point we concern ourselves with is: who was there to have it? Was there a watcher? Who, as the venerable Rinzai pointed out, is 'the master behind all the experiences'?

Here, very forthrightly, is the Fourth Patriarch of Zen: "The practice of bodhisattvas has Emptiness as its Realization. When beginners see Emptiness, this is 'seeing' Emptiness, it is not real Emptiness. Those who cultivate the way and attain real Emptiness do not see Emptiness or non-Emptiness; they have no views."

Therefore, in Zen we talk of 'Enlightenment Realization' or simply, Realization.

This is what Awakening connotes: awareness, insight, consciousness, self-transformation.

How does one articulate the unutterable? An evocative articulation of Realization in Zen came from Ch'an Master Wei-hsin of Ch'ing-yuan Mountain. He said to his disciples: "Thirty years ago, before I underwent training, I saw mountains as mountains and rivers as rivers. After I had called on Enlightened persons, I managed to enter Ch'an and saw mountains were not mountains and rivers were not rivers. Now that I have stopped (my false thinking), I see mountains are mountains and rivers are rivers."

And so the most famous Zen lines of Realization are these:

Before Enlightenment, mountains are mountains, rivers are rivers.
During Enlightenment, mountains are not mountains, rivers are not rivers.
After Enlightenment, mountains are mountains, rivers are rivers.

In the unawakened state, *mountains are mountains, rivers are rivers.* You are you, I am I, god is in heaven, humans on earth. Humans, god, Buddha-nature, self, ego, all are substantial realities standing distinct from each other, keeping their separate identities and domains. One's identity is vis-à-vis the others. The problem arises in our investment in attachment to such identities. Zen calls this state one of "greed, hatred and illusion". It is the world of *samsara*, the world of delusion. It is basically a world centred on oneself, an ego-centric world.

In the first stage of Awakening, where *mountains are not mountains, rivers are not rivers*, there takes place a withdrawal of projections. We let go of our ego-self, transcend its boundaries and limitations and suddenly we realize that all our ideas, concepts, images of ultimate reality, god, Self, Buddha-nature and their differentiation and separation are just objectification and imagination of the Something that is beyond imagination and objectification. With this realization our world as we see it, in terms of subject and object, I and god, collapses. With that goes our sense of security based on such objects. Our ego has become de-centred.

Reality is not out there, Buddha-nature is not a thing. You cannot prove any of these ultimate realities, you cannot see and touch them, they are not objects among objects of the world. There is no 'hard reality' to these concepts; they turn out to be phantoms of the mind. Rinzai described this state as the First Procedure where "Environment is taken away, Man is left."

There are no objects out there in the state of beyond-the-ego-self! No god, no Buddha, no things. The ground has been swept away from under your feet. This is the stage of 'If you meet the Buddha, kill him', 'if you meet god, kill him'. Letting go of all objectification of ultimate reality, you stand on your own feet, you stand alone in the affirmation: 'I alone am the Holy One'.

You throw away all the oppressive idols and concepts of gods.

In the next phase you Awaken to the realization that there is no ground in yourself, either. Your sense of who and what you are has so far been grounded in relation to the world and to the others; even, in a sense, in the absence of the other. You realize that the sense of your secure self is only a dream, a phantom, an illusion. You now see that what you know as your self is only a conflicted, discontinuous, endless appearing and disappearing of sensations, ideas, images and emotions. Utter groundlessness. No thing to hold on to. "Man and environment are taken away," to use Rinzai's Third Procedure. One may desperately try to take control. But the only safety and security is to let go controlling and seeking securities. One has to learn to let go and surrender. No manipulations, no achieving and no controlling; no attachments, no running away: only non-doing; letting-be.

One enters then into the 'Dark Night'. It is the beginning of the realization that one really does not know what ultimate reality is, what Buddha-nature, or the self, or god, or the world ultimately is.

Not only god, Buddha-nature, or Nirvana, but the Self, too, is unknowable and ineffable. The Self is empty. Emperor Wu of Liang asked Bodhidharma, "Who are you?" Bodhidharma replied, "I don't know." Buddhas and Patriarchs don't know it; sun and moon do not shine on it. Not only the Self, but each and everything is ultimately "I don't know", a darkness and mystery. It is the realization of utter groundlessness, the Emptiness of the Self and the Emptiness of all dharmas or things. "From the beginning, there is nothing at all."

Transpersonal psychologist Ken Wilber explains: "Enlightenment is not 'omniscience' but 'ascience'—not all-knowing but not-knowing—the utter release from the cramp of knowledge, which is always the world of form, when all you are in truth is formless. Not the cloud of knowing, but the cloud of unknowing. Not divine knowledge, but divine ignorance. The Seer *cannot* be seen; the Knower *cannot* be known; the Witness *cannot* be witnessed. What you are therefore is just a free fall in divine ignorance, a vast Freedom from all things known and heard and felt, an infinity of Freedom..."

It is not mere intellectual understanding, not mere ignorance. At first it feels like a negative and frightening void; but as one enters this darkness and surrenders oneself into the mystery, the darkness itself becomes light and grace. From this Emptiness stream forth the ten thousand dharmas. The self is affirmed unconditionally, let-be, and *thus* is each and everything. It is the self and the world transformed.

It is said of Hogen that when he was driven to a corner in his effort to understand ultimate reality he said to the master, "O master! I am now in a situation in which language is reduced to silence and thinking has no way to follow." The master remarked, "If you still are to talk about ultimate reality, see how it is nakedly apparent in everything and every event!" Each and everything *presents* itself. The *suchness* of reality, the *isness* of each and everything, is the presentation of Emptiness.

Emptiness can mean many things: particularly self-emptying, letting go, dying; entering into darkness and unknowing; the suchness and *isness* of beings. It should not be identified with a condition or a state of mind; it is not a thing, nor the state of unity as against multiplicity.

Emptiness is beyond all language and words, and it is at the same time all language and words. "As to what stands prior to the Word, not one phrase has been handed down even by the thousand holy ones," said Engo Zenji. It is one and many, duality and non-duality, thinking and non-thinking, spontaneity and constraint. It is negation of everything and resurrection of all. "The world is not the world, therefore the world is the world." In Emptiness, there is neither self nor the world and, at the same time, Emptiness is the ten thousand things. "Form is Emptiness; Emptiness is Form," says the Heart Sutra. It is not a matter of standing apart and 'knowing Emptiness', because that would still imply a subject-object split. It is a matter of losing one's whole self and in that dying, finding oneself in Mystery that is graciousness.

Let me give you a *koan*.

> *In a well that has not been dug, water is rippling from a spring that does not flow; there, someone with no shadow or form is drawing the water.*

Who is that without shadow or form who is drawing water? How does the water flow from a well not dug? Whence comes the spring that does not flow?

Not One, Not Two

> *A monk asked Isan, "What is Tao?"*
> *Isan replied, "Mindlessness is Tao."*
> *The monk said, "I do not comprehend!"*
> *"All you need is to apprehend the one who does not comprehend!"*
> *"Who is the one who does not comprehend?"*
> *"He is none other than yourself."*

Isan's disciple Kyozan Awakened on hearing about the divine spark in oneself.

> *Kyozan asked, "What is the abiding place of the true Buddha?"*
> *Isan replied, "By the ineffable subtlety of thinking without thinking, turn your attention inwards to reflect on the infinite power of the divine spark. When your thinking can go no further, it returns to its source, where Nature and Form eternally abide, where phenomenon and noumenon are not dual but one. It is there that abides the suchness of the true Buddha."*

This Formless Self is intuited and realized in and through the ego-self: the two are one and not-one. Awakened, we move in awareness between the two. We are aware of the Formless Self as our own ground and depth and yet we are also aware of discontinuity.

Seiichi Yagi, explaining this dual structure of consciousness, comments on Zen Master Hisamatsu: "Although Hisamatsu maintained that the Formless was the self and self was the Formless, he also held that to be 'I' possessed structure and articulation. He could speak directly from the Formless within him. When he said 'I do', it meant that the Formless acted through his empirical ego, but at the same time as his empirical ego, for the Formless expresses itself only through the empirical ego—that is the ego that is Awakened to the Formless. And because the Formless is immortal, he could say, 'I do not die'."

This Formless Self is boundless openness, unbounded and undefined, an expanseless expanse, a limitless spaciousness. This Self is transparent to all the world, *is* all the world. A bird chirps, it is the chirping of the boundless Self; a tree is seen, the tree is the presentation of the Formless Self. In this Formless Self, knowing and known are not two separate entities. At the same time, one can be in one's own unique ego-self standing apart and separate.

We can speak of a threefold relationship: I-It, I-Thou and I-I.

I-It is the relation of subject-object. I-Thou is one of face to face. The I-I relationship is coincidence of face over face, of total love in total union: it is I AM in I AM.

The Hindu sage Sadasiva wrote, "I can find no corner within my heart where I may take a stand to worship him, for in every 'I' which I attempt to utter, his 'I' is already glowing."

The Self moves freely in this threefold relationship. The Self is not to be confined only to the I-I relationship, or to the Formless aspect alone. It is one and many, dual and non-dual and also neither. It is not simply my self, nor your self. It is I *and* not-I, self *and* other. It is I-I, it is also I-with-you. When you see a tree, you are the tree, when you hear a sound, you are the sound. You can say then that there is no self. You can say also that the self has been opened up, it is now a boundless openness and that each and everything can let-be in this boundless openness, which is but the presenting of Reality itself.

I am the tree; I am the sound. But rarely is there such an awareness without a remainder. Even if I am only aware of being the tree and of nothing else for the moment, I soon come back to a dual awareness—of being a tree, and also of knowing that I am the tree. This being, and being-aware-of, is a being-with awareness. For a brief while 'I' am lost, and then 'I' come back, to stand as self-and-other. It is not a knowing of an object, but a knowing-with, and a being-with. It is I *and* not-I, phenomenon and noumenon, empty and full, paradoxical and mysterious. The self-enclosed self, the ego-self enclosed on itself, has been opened up, to realize itself as all the world. It is I and not-I, I-I and I-with-Thou.

From conception to birth, in living and until death, the human being is an inter-being, brought forth in love, led forth by love into love; all of one's being and life is a process of self-giving and self-receiving. Do not reduce Reality to the one-dimensional 'I alone'. This 'I alone' is only the ego-I.

The other as object, the other as total and alien other, is the ego level, the unawakened level of "trees are trees, mountains are mountains". In the unawakened state the ego tries to reduce all to itself, to expand and absorb all into itself or to be absorbed by the other; all others are reduced to objects and slaves, all are swallowed up by the ego, which finally destroys itself. Whereas, the Awakened is not-one, not-two, it is one and many.

True Awakening is to come to a Realization of the not-one, not-many, the Self manifesting as the many. Master Tozan Ryokai's levels of Awakening show us the way. Tozan's master was Ungan. When he reached a deep state of Realization, Tozan composed the following poem:

> *How wonderful! How wonderful!*
> *The inanimate expounding the Dharma*
> *What an ineffable truth!*
> *If you try to hear it with your ears,*
> *You will never understand it.*
> *Only when you hear it with your eyes.*
> *Will you really know it.*

This is a great Enlightenment poem, which shows Tozan having broken through to the beyond-of-ego. When Tozan was taking leave of Ungan, he asked the master, "After you have completed this life, what shall I say if anyone asks, 'Can you still recall your master's true face?' " The master remained silent for a long while and then replied, "Just this one is!" Carrying these words in his mind, Tozan travelled along; later, in crossing a stream, he happened to see his own reflection in the water and Awakened to the real meaning of "Just this one is". He expressed it in a *gatha*:

> *Do not seek him anywhere else!*
> *Or he will run away from you!*
> *Now that I go on all alone,*
> *I meet him everywhere.*
> *He is even now what I am.*
> *I am even now not what he is.*
> *Only by understanding this way,*
> *Can there be a true union with the Self-So.*

This *gatha* brings out beautifully Tozan's deeper and further stages of Awakening. It is not enough to hear the inanimate expounding the Dharma, not enough to hear with the eyes and see with the ears; you have to meet 'him' wherever you go and he is you but you are not he. The self is I-I, as well as I and not-I.

Once Kyozan inquired about his junior co-disciple Kyogen's level of Realization. Kyogen composed a *gatha*:

> Last year's poverty was not real poverty;
> This year's poverty is poverty indeed.
> Poor as I was last year,
> I still possessed enough ground to stand an awl on.
> This year I am so poor
> That I do not even have an awl.

Kyozan remarked that this *gatha* showed that Kyogen had attained 'Tathagatha Chan' and not yet 'Patriarchal Chan', that is, he was not yet fully realized. The above poem points to utter poverty and emptiness. But this is still not final Awakening. Kyogen later composed another *gatha*:

> I have an innate aptitude
> To look at him by a twinkle
> If anyone does not understand this,
> Let him not call himself a sramana!

Kyozan now approved of him as having attained Patriarchal Chan or complete Awakening.

Only when you Awaken to this dimension are you truly Awakened. Only then do you truly come home. 'I' then becomes an opening as well as a presence to all times and to all beings. A monk asked Chan Khong. "What is illumination?" Chan Khong replied, "Illumination shines through the whole world (revealing that) all sentient beings are together in a single family."

There is a *koan* that goes like this:

> Master Zuigan called to himself everyday, "Master!" and answered, "Yes, sir!" Then he would say,

"Be wide awake!" and answer, *"Yes, sir!" "Henceforward, never be deceived by others!" "No, I won't."*

Who is the master who calls? Who is the master who answers? Who deceives whom?

Mountains are Mountains, Rivers are Rivers

I have tried to articulate the inner movements and dynamics of Awakening and its different phases. Such articulation in language is not itself Awakening; but such articulation is essential. The letter alone kills, but the spirit needs the letter. Such articulation allows us to see whether Awakening is partial or full, one-dimensional or many dimensional.

I very often see people, particularly Zen teachers, stuck in the first few levels. There is a real danger in becoming too attached to our ideas of True Self. We then divide ourselves too much into the so-called ego-self and the True Self; we work hard to get ourselves into the 'heavenly' mode or get stuck onto one pole, whether we call it *samadhi*, or openness, or oneness, or Self, etc. Attachment to oneness and openness, to True Self or to Emptiness, is also delusion and egoism. Mumon puts it elegantly in his verse to the *koan, Zuigan Calls His Master:*

> *Clinging to the deluded way of consciousness,*
> *Students of the way do not realize truth.*
> *The seed of birth and death through endless eons:*
> *The fool calls it the true original self*

The fashion today, especially on the bestseller lists, is that of living in the Awareness of the Now. This is actually an essential practice. When Sakyamuni Buddha was once asked what he did, he is believed to have said: "When I walk, I walk; when I eat, I eat; when I sleep, I sleep." It was the Buddha's way of showing us the practice of mindfulness. Following the popularization of the memorable quote we now have scores of books telling us that the essence of Buddhist practice is to "eat when you eat, shit when you shit". This can, unfortunately, be a mask for an unawakened practice. Because the people who are telling you this are not pointing you to the ultimate teachings of the Buddha, to the realm of the beyond-awareness, and the beyond-present.

Engo Zenji, the famous 12th century commentator of *The Blue Cliff Record* (*Hekiganroku*), illustrates this clearly, in his comment on case 9:

"Some people say, 'Fundamentally there isn't the slightest bit of anything, but when we have tea we drink tea, and when we have rice we eat rice'. This is big vain talk; I call this claiming attainment without having attained, claiming Realization without having realized... (those who say so) are far from knowing that before the Patriarch came, people scarcely called the sky earth, or called mountains rivers; why did the Patriarch still come from the West?"

All this leads me to believe that the 'ascent' in Zen, where one kills the Buddha and the Patriarchs, meaning the negation of all concepts and attachments, is comparatively easy. It is the 'descent' that is hard: the descent into the many, the other, the being-with.

In the ultimate level, there is nothing at all, it is empty. In the phenomenal level, everything is alive, everything different and unique. How do we reconcile the two?

True Awakening, as we saw, easily reconciles the One and the many. When the Awakening is partial, the understanding superficial, the dangers and pitfalls are many. Zen has been denigrated, and rightly so I would say, when its proponents have played around with literalisms. One doctor, who prided himself on his 'Enlightenment', is reported to have told a patient who was having high fever, "There is no sickness at all, what do you want medicine for?" He didn't know that being sick is itself manifestation of Emptiness, and that in dealing with sickness appropriately as a doctor, he was called to actualize Buddha-nature. A Japanese Zen master is said to have lectured soldiers during World War II that since there is no-self, there is none who kills and none who is killed, and therefore when ordered to shoot their response should be to go bang-bang. This is confusing the ultimate level with the phenomenal level and shows ethical blindness. Immorality and self-indulgence are thus sought to be justified.

It reminds me of a Zen story. Yamaoka Tesshu, as a young student of Zen, visited one master after another. He called upon Dokuon of Shokoku. To show his attainment, he said, "The mind, Buddha and sentient beings, after all, do not exist. The true nature of phenomena is Emptiness. There is no Realization, no delusion, no sage, no mediocrity. There is no giving and nothing to be received." Dokuon, who was smoking quietly, said nothing. Suddenly he whacked Yamaoka with his bamboo pipe. This made the youth quite angry. "If nothing exists," inquired Dokuon, "where did this anger come from?"

Zen language like 'suchness is discrimination, discrimination is suchness' can become oppressive language. This has made some Zen scholars declare that 'Zen is not Buddhism', since Zen seems to discourage in ordinary life discrimination and ethics that are central to Buddhism. This is a result of confusing the different levels of language; of reducing Zen language to the literal, which itself comes from inadequate or immature Realization or Awakening.

I would like to dwell on this problem a little. To clear our misunderstandings I would like to take you back to some of the core teachings of Buddhism, specifically the teaching of the Two Truths. In the words of Nagarjuna, "The teaching of the doctrine of the Buddha is based upon two truths: the truth of worldly convention (*samvriti*) and, the ultimate, supreme truth (*paramartha*). Those who do not discern the distinction between these two truths do not understand the profound nature of the Buddha's teaching."

The distinction is not one of metaphysics, but one of language and experience. There are different forms of language: moral-ethical, doxological-liturgical, practical, scientific, mathematical, business, love, etc. One cannot simply interchange one for another. The exterior language of Zen, also that of Christianity for that matter—the symbols, rituals, teachings, structures—are the 'body'; the interior, or spiritual, path is the journey of 'soul-making'. I am very taken by the comment of Simone Weil: "When genuine friends of god—such as was Eckhart, to my way of thinking—repeat words they have heard in secret amidst the silence of union of love, and these words are in disagreement with the teaching of the Church, it is simply that the language of the marketplace is not that of the nuptial chamber."

The dangers that I have so far discussed are also the dangers that we face in *koan* work, which often brings us to a Realization of 'Just This'.

There is a *koan* where Joshu is seen struggling with discriminating the Way and identifying himself with it; Nansen shatters all his attachments and dualisms:

> *Joshu asked Nansen, "What is the Way?" Nansen replied, "The ordinary mind is the Way." Joshu asked, "Should I direct myself towards it or not?" Nansen said, "If you try to turn towards it, you go against it."*

> Joshu asked, "If I do not try to turn towards it, how can I know that it is the Way?" Nansen answered, "The Way does not belong to knowing or not-knowing. Knowing is delusion; not-knowing is blank consciousness. When you have really reached the true Way beyond all doubt, you will find it as vast and boundless as outer space. How can it be talked about on a level of right and wrong?"

Here is another *koan*:

> A monk told Joshu, "I have just entered the monastery. Please teach me."
> Joshu asked, "Have you eaten your rice porridge?"
> The monk replied, "I have eaten."
> Joshu said, "Then you had better wash your bowl."
> At that moment the monk was Enlightened.

All these *koans* bring you to 'Just this, Just this!' There are no secrets in Zen; the truth is manifest before your very eyes. The flower is red, the leaves green, the sun shines, the bird sings. 'Just this, Just this.' But what is this 'Just this'? There is a temptation among Zen practitioners to take this as 'Just this, nothing more!' "Eating, washing, getting up, sitting down that is all, nothing more. Look out, what you see is Buddha-nature, is Reality, *nothing more.*"

So what is the meaning of the last line of our Zen verse, *After Enlightenment, mountains are mountains, rivers are rivers?*

The last phase of 'mountains are mountains, rivers are rivers' *contains within it,* 'mountains are not mountains, rivers are not rivers'.

Madhyamika's Fourfold Logic (*catuskoti*) puts it like this: It can be said of a being that it (1) is, (2) is not, (3) both is and is not, and (4) neither is nor is not.

Illustrating this, Nagarjuna declared:

Everything is suchness
Everything is not suchness
Everything is both suchness and not suchness
Everything is neither suchness nor not suchness.

The first line affirms the existence of all dharmas or beings; this is worldly truth, *samvriti satya*. The second denies or negates the self-substantial existence of all beings; this is ultimate truth, *paramartha satya*. It is Emptiness. The third combines the world of being and that of Emptiness. The fourth negates and transcends the third. This last phase is said to be the liberating path, the Middle Way. However, Truth, and Zen, are not bound by this either; they also negate all four alternatives as description of the truth of beings.

Let us try to understand all this in the light of the 'just this' of *After Enlightenment, mountains are mountains, rivers are rivers*. When we say 'just this', this 'just this' contains at its heart 'not this'. Otherwise, it is mere worldly truth. The same applies to 'Samsara is Nirvana, Nirvana is Samsara'; or 'Form is Emptiness, Emptiness is Form'. Form is Emptiness only when Form has been negated and transcended. Only when you have gone beyond both is and is-not, can you truly say 'just this'. If you take 'just this' as *literally* only this and nothing more, it is a merely materialistic, literalistic, self-enclosed ego consciousness. Literalism kills truth, kills the soul. 'Just this' to be truly 'just this', includes the 'not this', and only then the 'just this' can manifest mountains, rivers, the sun and the stars, and the whole universe itself.

All these terms—manyness and oneness, identity and non-identity, immanence and transcendence, being and non-being—are not be taken as static, literal realities. They are symbols and ciphers, inviting one to action. Being is actualized action; action means feeling, thinking, judging, choosing, doing and these take place in an act of response.

When I take the pen and write, is it the pen that writes? Or my hand? Or I? Or the universe? Are these one or two?

Here is a *koan* from the *Blue Cliff Record*:

> *Riku Taifu, while talking to Nansen, said, "Jo Hosshi said, 'Heaven and earth are of the same root. All things and I are of one substance.' Isn't that absolutely fantastic?" Nansen pointed to a flower in the garden, called Taifu to him and said, "People of these days see this flower as though they are in a dream."*

Setcho's verse on the *koan*:

> *Hearing, seeing, touching and knowing are not one and one;*
> *Mountains and rivers should not be viewed in the mirror.*
> *The frosty sky, the setting moon—at midnight;*
> *With whom will the serene waters of the lake reflect the shadows in the cold?*

A Brief History of Zen

Sometime in the 6th century. A young seeker stands resolutely in front of the old master that he has long sought and who is now glaring ferociously at him. It is an icy winter in northern China, the young man is knee-deep in snow outside the Shaolin Monastery on Mount Sung and shivering in the biting wind. The master sitting motionless and unresponsive in front of him is a foreigner, come from the far-off land of the sun in the west, speaking a strange tongue and following a fiercely uncompromising path to what he calls Enlightenment. Still, our young seeker is undeterred and continues to beseech the cantankerous old man to accept him as a student. The old man is unmoved. In a last, desperate measure, the young man cuts off his arm, offers it to the master and begs to be taught by him. The old man relents and takes him on as his disciple.

Our story doesn't end there, it continues. The disciple is still hounding his mentor, again with a heart-rending, impassioned entreaty. The old man sits gazing at a wall, and the student implores, "Your disciple's mind is not yet at peace. I beg you, my teacher, please give it peace." "Bring the mind to me," roars the old master, "and I will set it at rest." "I have searched for the mind," replies the dejected student, "and it is finally unattainable." "There," says the master, "I have thoroughly set it at rest for you." And in that moment, the student comes to sudden and great Awakening.

It's a gripping tale and probably apocryphal but the protagonists bear historical scrutiny. The old master was Bodhidharma, hailed as the founder of Zen Buddhism, and the seeker was his disciple and successor Hui-k'e, who became a well-known Zen master and was known as the Second Patriarch of Zen.

A Master, a Myth and a Metaphor

The history of Zen Buddhism can be narrated as a series of events (sometimes historically true, sometimes merely legendary) and processes that strung up a pan-cultural form of meditative practice; but its spirit is better understood when examined through the lives and attainments of the great masters whose personalities as much as their teachings lent muscle—and much drama—to the Zen ethos.

Zen history begins, then, with Bodhidharma, regarded as the First Patriarch of Zen. Not much is known about Bodhidharma, other than the fact that he arrived in China around 520 from south India, to spread his form of Mahayana-based Buddhist meditative practice. It came to be known as Ch'an, a corruption of the Sanskrit word for meditation, *dhyana*. (This would once again get corrupted as Zen, in Japan.) The earliest written record available about Bodhidharma is a biography authored by Tao-hsuan in 645. The author notes: "(He was)… the third son of a great Brahman king in South India, of the Western Lands. He was a man of wonderful intelligence, bright and far-reaching; he thoroughly understood everything that he ever learned. As his ambition was to master the doctrine of the Mahayana, he abandoned the white dress of the layman and put on the black robe of monkhood... He finally made up his mind to cross over land and sea and come to China and preach his doctrine in the kingdom of Wei." From south China, where he landed, Bodhidharma seems to have travelled to the northern districts and taught a meditation technique based on Mahayana. His teachings seem to have even brought him into conflict with the mainstream meditation teachers. By most accounts, he was executed just outside Luoyang during skirmishes in the northern Wei region sometime between 528 and 534.

These are the bare facts. Over the next six centuries, through the myth making of succeeding generations of teachers, masters and practitioners, Bodhidharma metamorphosed into a legendary and charismatic icon of Ch'an. The incidents between Bodhidharma and Hui-k'e mentioned earlier, for instance, appear in interpolated sections of ancient texts. (Hui-k'e more likely lost his arm to highway bandits who were known to inflict this form of torture on their victims in the China of those times.) From the irrepressible Shen-hui (684-758) came the anointing of Bodhidharma as the First Patriarch of Zen in China. Sitting in his monastery in Ho-tse, Shen-hui traced (or more precisely, fabricated) a lineage of masters of the dharma, starting with Sakyamuni Buddha himself as the First Patriarch in India and Mahakashyapa, known from historical records as the foremost disciple of the Buddha, as Second Patriarch. The story, avidly pushed by Shen-hui, goes: the Buddha was speaking to a large gathering when, realizing that his disciple's mind had reached the critical point that could lead to Awakening, he suddenly held up a flower and smiled. In that instant Mahakashyapa was Enlightened, and as the receiver of the 'transmission of the Buddha-mind' he became his successor and the Second Patriarch in India. Shen-hui drew up a list of 28 successive Patriarchs (unacknowledged as such in Indian sources and records), one in each generation. Shen-hui identified Bodhidharma as the 28th Patriarch in India, and later the First Patriarch of Ch'an in China. Other stories appeared in interpolated texts: as, for example, the famed encounter with Emperor Wu of the Liang dynasty that unambiguously states the Mahayana doctrine of Emptiness:

> *Said Emperor Wu, "Ever since the beginning of my reign I have built so many temples, copied so many sacred books, and supported so many sacred monks and nuns; what do you think my merit might be?"*
> *"No merit whatever, Sire!" Bodhidharma replied.*
> *"Why?" demanded the Emperor.*
> *"All these are inferior deeds that would cause their author to be born in the heavens or on this earth again. They still show traces of worldliness, they are like shadows following an object…"*
> *"What then is the first principle of the holy doctrine?" the Emperor asked.*
> *"Vast Emptiness and there is nothing in it to be called holy."*
> *"Who is it then who is now confronting me?"*
> *"I know not."*

To Bodhidharma is attributed the famous verse that is unparalleled in its embodiment of the essence of Ch'an and was actually written long after the grand old man's death:

> *A special transmission outside the scriptures*
> *Not founded upon words and letters;*
> *By pointing directly to (one's) mind*

> *It lets one see into (one's own true) nature and (thus) attain Buddhahood.*

Buddhist meditation was well established in China by the time Bodhidharma reached its shores. Buddhism had, in many ways, found more fertile ground to grow in China, where Taoism was deep-rooted, than even in its country of origin. Writes historian Heinrich Dumoulin: "Whereas the Indians were inhibited by their agonizing struggle for salvation, the Chinese, who desired nothing so much as to penetrate the secrets of nature, abandoned themselves completely to the Taoist-Buddhist naturalism." As early as the first century, the *Lankavatara Sutra*, which presupposes the Ch'an principle of not relying on words and teachings but directly examining one's own mind to attain Enlightenment, was known in China. In the one and only text (*Two Entrances and Four Acts*) of Bodhidharma's available to us, he uses the term *pi-kuan*, literally 'wall-gazing', that became pivotal in the establishment of Ch'an practice and its distinctive recognition of Enlightenment. The term 'wall-gazing' came to mean not only the practice of long meditation but also the sudden and penetrating Enlightenment that it could afford. It was also this term from which grew the legend of Bodhidharma sitting gazing at a wall for nine years until his legs withered away.

All the myths do not, however, take away from the singular importance of Bodhidharma's arrival in China. The myths served a purpose, which was to show, in as spectacular a manner as possible, the originality and freshness of his approach to the meditative discipline. Says scholar Yanagida, "...(Bodhidharma) symbolized the essence of Zen in the form of an idealized, unreachable model. Followers of Zen can extrapolate from the image of Bodhidharma the inner content of the way to Enlightenment." The image of the fierce master transformed itself into a cipher in *koan* practice. To this day, Zen students are asked the *koan*, "What is the meaning of Bodhidharma coming from the West?" It is a way of asking, "What is the meaning of Zen?"

The Patriarchs of Zen

As the Second Patriarch, Hui-k'e led the life of a wandering ascetic, as did his successor and the Third Patriarch Seng-t'san. Very little is known about the latter, but his one legacy is the Zen poem *On Believing in the Mind*, breathtaking in its vision, its brilliance and clarity of thought. (Some scholars doubt that he wrote it but he did seem to have recited it often to his disciples.) The Fourth Patriarch, the scholarly Tao-hsin (580-651), gave up the life of a mendicant and chose instead to settle down with his disciples in a monastery on Shuan-feng Mountain, where he lived for 30 years and is believed to have led over 500 students on the path to Enlightenment. This settling down was an important transition that paved the way for the formal Zen practices of later generations. Tao-hsin himself was known to have sat day and night in meditation, but he encouraged his monks to continue their practice even while engaging in the daily activities of community life.

After Tao-hsin came Hung-jen, the Fifth Patriarch. The foundation would now be laid for the high drama, amazing antics and stories of sudden Enlightenment and penetrating insights that would characterize the Ch'an school and carve its image of robust iconoclasm. Hung-jen perfected the community life and work-as-practice Ch'an that Tao-hsin began. He, too, would participate in community activities during the day and meditate from dusk to dawn. Hung-jen's achievements were considerable but in the annals of Zen history he became best known for his spotting of his celebrated successor Hui-neng, the Sixth Patriarch of Ch'an.

It was time for Fifth Patriarch Hung-jen to find his successor. He asked his monks to compose a verse

> *manifesting their Enlightenment. The leader of the monks, Shen-hsiu, composed his verse and put it up on the monastery wall:*
>
>> *The body is the Bodhi tree,*
>> *The mind is a clear mirror stand.*
>> *Wipe it clean moment by moment*
>> *Never let dust and rubbish adhere to it.*
>
> *The verse clearly portrays Shen-hsiu's 'gradual approach' to Enlightenment. Layman Hui-neng, then a cook in the monastery's kitchen, heard of this and countered it with his own verse:*
>
>> *The Bodhi is intrinsically no tree;*
>> *Nor has the clear mirror any stand.*
>> *There is not one thing from the beginning,*
>> *Where can dust and rubbish adhere at all?*
>
> *Seeing this verse, the Fifth Patriarch went to the kitchens, called for Hui-neng, gave him thirty blows and also his robe and bowl (symbols of 'transmission'), and named him his successor. But alive to the possibility of a revolt within the ranks of the monk community at this elevation of a lay person, he advised Hui-neng to leave the monastery under cover of darkness that very night, polish his Enlightenment in solitude for a few years and, when the time was ripe, return to assume his true role as the Sixth Patriarch of Zen.*

This story, too, is apocryphal. In fact, it is thought to have been made up by Hui-neng's disciple Shen-hui to establish the supremacy of the method of 'sudden Enlightenment' over that of 'gradual Enlightenment'.

Thus have legend and fact become hopelessly intertwined in the story of the succession of Hui-neng. The facts that scholars have been able to sift are that Hui-neng, not yet a monk but a layman in the monastery of Hung-jen, was named Sixth Patriarch over the hitherto favoured Shen-hsiu in somewhat secret fashion by the master, that immediately following this he left the monastery, lived a solitary life in the mountains refining his spiritual attainments for the next 16 years and only then took ordainment as monk, and his due mantle and title as Sixth Patriarch.

In Zen history, Hui-neng is accorded a status equal to that of Bodhidharma, in fact he is even described as the true founder of Zen. This pre-eminent stature was accorded to him by the numerous Ch'an masters who later declared their complete allegiance to his teachings. He came to be known after his death as the Zen Master of the Great Mirror. The Enlightened Mind is experienced suddenly, he taught, and to realize it no special exercises of concentration are necessary. "The mind is one and, like a mirror, is in motionless repose and yet perpetually active, for its brightness reflects continuously." Basing his teachings on Mahayana texts, particularly the Diamond Sutra, he delivered the famed *Sutra Spoken by the Sixth Patriarch from the High Seat of the Gem of the Law*, popularly known as the Platform Sutra and regarded as *the* complete Zen doctrine of Enlightenment. In the sixty years that he taught, Hui-neng drew a large gathering of disciples.

Shen-hsiu, meanwhile, travelled north and there set up his own monastery and practice. Unlike Hui-neng, Shen-hsiu did not emphasize 'sudden Enlightenment' but preferred the method of gradual Enlightenment. Through constant practice, he maintained, one could gradually cleanse the mind of impurities so that the Original Mind could suddenly shine forth. While Hung-jen named Hui-neng his successor, he nevertheless had only the highest praise for Shen-hsiu and his method; historical records also suggest that Hui-neng and Shen-hsiu held each other in great esteem.

The influence of the Northern School, never too strong, pitted as it was against the teachings of the venerable Hui-neng, soon declined. After the death of Hui-neng, the Ch'an Patriarchate came to an end. Many disciples became Zen masters themselves, establishing their own following.

One long, dynamic chapter in Zen history may have ended but what was to follow was a resoundingly triumphant leap of faith, spiritual attainment and its imaginative articulation, of an order and magnitude never before or after seen in the history of world religions.

The 'Mad' Masters of Zen

Notes Dumoulin, "The period from the death of Hui-neng in 713 until the persecution of Buddhism under Emperor Wu-tsung (845) was the Golden Age of Chinese Zen, on which the chronicles, sayings and *koan* collections of later times present almost unlimited material… (The) Enlightened masters (of this period) burn Buddha images and *sutras*, laugh in the face of inquirers or suddenly shout at them, and indulge in a thousand absurdities. Though they may behave like fools and possess nothing, yet they feel themselves true kings in their free mastery of Enlightenment. They know no fear, since they desire nothing and have nothing to lose."

Full of sound and fury, and bristling with their spiritual advancement, each of these masters devised his own eccentric method of teaching, some of which are followed in sanitized form in Zen centres to this day. Here's an ancient text on the redoubtable Ma-tsu (707-786), precursor of the powerful Rinzai sect of Zen: "His appearance was remarkable. He strode along like a bull and glared about him like a tiger. If he stretched out his tongue, it reached over his nose; on the soles of his feet were imprinted two circular marks." He was the first to use the Zen shout *katz!* to jolt students to an Awakening. Pronounced '*Ka-aa-aaa*', the shout continues to be used extensively by Zen masters seeking to empty disciples' minds of concepts and doctrines. Ma-tsu was also one of the first to extensively use paradoxical utterances to challenge aspirants. After one such paradoxical dialogue, he is known to have twisted the nose of his student Pai-chang so hard that the latter let out a sharp cry—and was jolted into Enlightenment! For all this 'madness', Ma-tsu was a great master and declared what is virtually the Zen mantra: "Apart from the mind there is no Buddha, and apart from the Buddha there is no mind."

Ma-tsu's student Nansen perfected the art of the paradox, but it was his own student Joshu who seems to have been the true king of the Zen paradox. Living up to the age of 120, Joshu prodded, challenged, coaxed, frustrated, puzzled and finally led to Enlightenment scores of seekers with brilliant repartees that showed the emptiness of words and pointed to the vital *nowness* or *isness* of Enlightenment.

> *A monk asked Joshu, "If a poor man comes, what should one give him?" The master answered, "He lacks nothing."*
>
> *A monk asked Joshu, "The ten thousand dharmas return to the One. Where does the One return?" The master replied, "While I was staying at Ch'ing-chou I made a robe that weighed seven pounds."*

And the most famous such encounter in the history of Zen, made so by its repeated reference and use as a *koan* in Zen centres to the present day:

> *A monk asked Joshu, "Does a dog have Buddha-nature or not?" Joshu replied, "Mu." (Mu means no, or not.)*

The Enlightenment story of Zen Master Te-shan (780-865) is as picturesque an illustration as we can get of the various means employed by Ch'an masters to prod seekers' mind to Realization. Well versed in Buddhist texts, Te-shan was a champion of *sutra* studies, but curiosity about the 'sudden Enlightenment' practices of the Southern School saw him wending his way south. On the way, a woman at a teashop asked him of the Diamond Sutra he was carrying: "In the commentaries it is written, 'the consciousness of the past is inexpressible, the consciousness of the present is inexpressible, the consciousness of the future is inexpressible.' What consciousness do you want to refresh?" She then directed the dumbstruck scholar to the monastery of Master Ch'ung-shin, five miles away in Lung-tan. Te-shan started practice there. Late one afternoon the master and the disciple were engaged in a long, deep discussion. His mind pushed to its very limits, Te-shan paused and looked out of the window. "It is dark," he said. Chung-shin lit a candle and handed it over. As Te-shan took the candle, the master blew it out. In that instant, Te-shan 'saw' and was Awakened. Next morning, he burnt all his *sutras*.

Chung-shin's successor as head of the Lung-tan monastery and a great Zen Master, Te-shan never assumed his seat in the meditation hall without a short stick with which he gave hard blows to his students to spur them on the path. "If you say a word," he would shout deafeningly, "thirty blows; if you don't say a word, thirty blows." A modified version of this practice is still followed in Zen centres today, in the form of the *kyosaku/keisaku*, a wooden paddle with which meditators' shoulders are struck (on request), to bring their mind to alertness.

Two of the most flamboyant masters of the period, who established their own schools of Zen, were Unmon (of the lineage of

Te-shan) and Rinzai. Unmon first practised with Zen Master Mu-chou. In true Zen tradition, thrice Unmon sought Enlightenment from his master and was thrice rebuffed. The third time, as the master threw him out of the door and shut it suddenly with tremendous force, Unmon's leg got caught in it and broke. With a yell of sheer pain, Unmon came to a sudden Enlightenment! As a Zen Master, Unmon meted the same treatment to his disciples, terrifying them with sudden deafening shouts and hard blows with his staff.

Unmon's original and lasting contribution to the Zen method was his habit of giving one-word answers to questions concerning Enlightenment. This came to be known as "the pass of the single word". Here's a sample:

> "What is the meaning of the Patriarch coming from the West?"
> "Master!"

Unmon also employed his predecessors' practice of exchanging trenchant dialogues and paradoxes with incisive results. He is best known for the following dialogue:

> *Unmon asked, "I do not ask you what was fifteen days past. But can you say a word about what will be fifteen days hence?" He gave the answer himself:*
> *"Every day is a good day."*

There were, by this time, five different streams of Zen, known as the Five Houses of Zen. Of those, the one that survived the longest was that of the towering Zen Master Lin-chi, better known by his Japanese name Rinzai. As a young man, Rinzai was literally beaten and pummeled into Enlightenment by his master. (In return, Rinzai 'showed' his Enlightenment to his master Ta-yu by poking him hard in the ribs.) Not surprisingly, these were his own methods as a master and to this day the Rinzai school is known as the strictest, most rigorous 'sudden Enlightenment' school of Zen. It is from this school that emerged the most sensational Zen stories of shouting and beatings in the meditation hall to goad students to a breakthrough.

Zen Sense, Zen Nonsense

By the 12th century Ch'an had started sliding into a state of decline in China, but two very important developments were to take place. One was the rising influence of the Tsao-tung sect (to be known famously, just a century later, as the Soto school in Japan), whose genesis lay in the teachings of Liang Chiai (Wu Pen) of Tung Shan Mountain, and his immediate successor Pen Chi of Ts'ao Shan Mountain in the late 9th and early 10th centuries. This school had developed the doctrine of 'silent illumination', and it now crystallized into its final form in the teachings of the great Zen Master Tien-t'ung (1091-1157). The master described the path as "knowing without touching the thing (known), and shining without forming an object". This is the method that is now known as 'just sitting', *shikantaza*, where the mind is not focused on any object but assumes the observer stance, until it sinks into awareness of itself. Tien-tung's contemporary in the Rinzai sect was Ta-hui, who perfected the other important development, the use of *koans*, "the great mockery of all rules of logic", as a means to Enlightenment.

During what Dumoulin graphically describes as "the time of the spiritual slackening", Zen adherents began to look back wistfully on the uproarious doings and stupendous attainments of the 'mad' masters of a bygone era. The masters had created a spiritual climate that propelled disciples on an independent path of enquiry that eventually led them back to their masters with critical questions that would bring them to an explosive Awakening. These 'encounters' and paradox-fraught dialogues were preceded by long periods (usually years) of hard practice on the part of the enquirer who would go to the master with his mind toughened to a state of single-pointed focus and tension. The master, sensing this, would deliver that critical response, that pregnant action or that timely blow that would shatter the tension and race the student past the 'gateless gate' of Realization.

Zen masters now began to use these recorded encounters in an effort to put disciples in the same state of mind as their forebears. The apparently meaningless or nonsensical dialogues and declarations were deliberately used to break the rationalization of the mind. To answer a *koan* the seeker would have to abandon all scriptural knowledge, analytical reasoning, experience—in short, abandon his mind—to become one with the *koan*, then transcend it. Collections of these encounters, called *kung-ans* or public cases, appeared, including the well-known *Wu-men-kuan* (in Japanese, *Mumonkan*) compiled by Wu-men (in Japanese, Mumon) and *Pi-yen-lu* (in Japanese, *Hekiganroku*) with commentaries by Engo and Setcho.

"Just steadily go on with your *koan* every moment of your life," Master Ta-hui advised his disciples, "...Whether walking or sitting, let your attention be fixed upon it without interruption... When all of a sudden something flashes out in your mind, its light will illumine the entire universe, and you will see the spiritual land of the Enlightened Ones fully revealed at the point of a single hair, and the great wheel of Dharma revolving in a single grain of dust."

Typically, the breakthrough (*satori* or *kensho*) that a student would achieve through the *koan* would be a glimpse of the True Self. He would then have to deepen this glimpse of Awakening by working on a series of *koans*. But recognition as an Enlightened person would be given only if his Realization was seen to be actualized in his everyday life—that is, if he was living the exemplary life, always in a state of openness and compassion. In time, this method has become systematized to become a 'course' of *koan* study, with students in Japan typically expected to 'pass' at least 500-1700 *koans* before they receive the 'seal of transmission' that would entitle them to be masters on their own.

Thus the two enduring mainstreams of Zen were firmly established, but the glory would now shift shores, to Japan, where the full, luminous flowering of Zen would take place under Masters Dogen and Hakuin.

Ch'an had, by then, already crossed Chinese shores and spread to southeast Asia. As far back as the 7th century, Ch'an travelled to Korea, where it came to be known as Sôn. The monk Pomnang travelled to China and trained with the Fourth Patriarch of Ch'an. His disciple Toui (783-821) is believed to be the first Korean monk to transmit the teachings of the Southern School's 'sudden Enlightenment'. This was further strengthened by the monk P'ou, who introduced Rinzai's methods. By far the most influential Sôn master, whose method continues to flourish to this day, was Chinul (1158-1210), who advocated the approach of sudden Enlightenment followed by gradual and simultaneous cultivation of insight or wisdom. But it was in Japan that Zen assumed the forms with which it is most associated today.

Drinking Tea, Eating Rice

Thirteenth century Japan. A boy of seven watches the incense from his mother's funeral services waft slowly up the Takao temple and reflects on the arising and decay of all things. Five years ago the boy had lost his father. At 12, rebelling against the worldly ambitions of his aristocratic uncle and fos-

ter father, he dons the robes of monkhood in a monastery devoted to Buddhist scriptural study at the foot of Mount Hei. Very soon, the scriptural studies fail to hold his interest and his mind is seized by the question, if we are intrinsically imbued with Buddha-nature, why do we need to seek it?

The search for the answer would take him to numerous masters and monasteries in Japan, across the seas to China where he would encounter fresh disciplines and practices and finally to the monastery of Master Ju-ching, successor of the great Tien-tung. In the 'silent illumination' Zen of Tien-tung his questions would finally find answer. He would sit night and day in meditation and one particular night, his mind in a state of complete dynamic stillness, he would hear the master loudly admonish a nodding fellow-meditator, "In Zen, body and mind are cast off, why do you sleep?" and would come to a great Awakening.

Back in Japan he would start his own monasteries, write a book that would sweep the imagination of an entire nation and through his teachings stride the world of Zen like a colossus.

The Zen world would be hard put to find a parallel to the influence and achievements of Zen Master Dogen Kigen (1200-1253), founder of the Soto school of Zen in Japan. Zen had made forays into Japan centuries before Dogen's first taste of Enlightenment in foreign land; the Rinzai school had already garnered a small following, but it was all still a fringe practice. Dogen brought it to centre stage. "Enlightenment is practice,

practice is Enlightenment," declared Dogen. To sit in meditation is not to *attain* Buddhahood but to *express* it. When you assume the posture of the Buddha you already are the Buddha. And so Dogen formulated a method of serene sitting, *zazen*, and a method of practice, *shikantaza*, which till today is the most widely practised form of Zen and which he detailed exhaustively in his magnum opus, *Shobogenzo*.

The sweep of both Soto and Rinzai Zen influence on Japanese culture from then on is nothing short of spectacular. From tea ceremonies to *haiku*, gardening to flower-arranging, fencing, wrestling, archery, the martial arts to calligraphy and painting, it permeated every aspect of life in Japan. Zen Masters like Muso, Ikkyu, and the haiku poet Basho contributed as much to its literature as to its growth and spread as a vigorous spiritual discipline. If the 'mad masters' of Ch'an articulated their Awakening in mind-bending paradoxes and comic action, the Zen masters of Japan expressed it in exquisite verse that showed the manifestation of Emptiness in the ordinary life of "drinking water, eating rice".

An old pond
A frog jumps in—
Plop!

exclaimed Basho in the most celebrated *haiku* of Enlightenment in the history of Zen. And so Enlightenment bloomed quietly, like a lotus in a still pond.

Like an Imbecile, Like an Idiot!

Five centuries later, the tranquil repose of Dogen's Zen had to contend with this great shout of Awakening from the great mystic of Zen, the venerable Hakuin (1685-1768). Hakuin's beginnings in the spiritual life were as dramatic as was his Awakening. As a boy, he was terrified of tales of hell and its torments, so learnt

Buddhist *sutras* to combat this fate (rendered possible, he thought, by his delight in killing insects and small birds), then tested the efficacy of his studies by applying a red-hot iron rod to his thigh. The *dharanis* of the Lotus Sutra (which he had studied) failed him, but his inner quest had begun. He chanced upon the story of the famous Rinzai Master Shih-shuang Ch'u-yuan "who meditated day and night without interruption and who, when threatened by drowsiness, bored his flesh with a sharp awl in order to arouse his mind with pain". Inspired, he threw himself into a fearsomely austere practice, meditating day and night on the *koan* "*Mu*".

An 'experience' happened and the excited Hakuin ("With a loud voice I called out, 'How glorious, how glorious' ") took off to report his Enlightenment to Master Dokyo Etan, who tested him and proclaimed: "You poor child of the devil in a dark dungeon!" Again and again, Hakuin went to him, again and again he was rebuffed with the same line and some rough treatment. Finally, as he was wandering around town with his begging bowl, Mu broke open and he came to an Awakening that laid him flat on the ground, literally. This time, Dokyo Etan stroked his back and confirmed his Enlightenment. Subsequently, Hakuin claimed to have had eleven Great Enlightenments and numerous small ones.

As a master in the Rinzai sect, Hakuin revived many of the practices of that school (the *koans*, the shouting and the beatings) and had a large following. "Once the Great Doubt arises," he wrote, "out of a hundred who practise, one hundred will achieve a breakthrough; and of one thousand, a thousand will break through."

Once again, and this time in Japan, both the schools of Zen (sudden Enlightenment and silent illumination, Rinzai and Soto) had come to full flowering. Formal practices were introduced, not only for monks but for lay people as well, making Zen

Buddhism the best structured meditation practice available today. They have helped Zen withstand the onslaughts of wars and modernization. In the later part of the 20th century, Zen once again crossed shores, this time to the far West (Europe and America), where it has adapted to new peoples and new cultures to keep ever fresh its roaring spirit, its gentle tranquillity.

List of Reading Material

Ciszek, Walter J. with Daniel Flaherty. *He Leadeth Me.* New York: Doubleday, 1973.

Cleary, Thomas. (Tr.) *Transmission of Light: Zen in the Art of Enlightenment by Zen Master Keizan.* San Franscisco: North Point Press, 1990.

Collins, Steven. *Nirvana and Other Buddhist Felicities.* Boston, Massachusetts: Cambridge University Press, 1999.

Conn, Walter E. *The Desiring Self.* New York/Mahwah, NJ: Paulist Press, 1998.

Dumoulin, Heinrich. *A History of Zen Buddhism.* New Delhi: Munshiram Manoharlal Publishers Pvt Ltd, 2000.

Goddard, Dwight. *The Teaching of Buddha, the Buddhist Bible: Buddha, Truth and Brotherhood; An Epitome of Many Buddhist Scriptures Translated from the Japanese.* Santa Barbara, California: Dwight Goddard, 1934.

Hillman, James. *Loose Ends.* Texas: Spring Publications, 1978

Hoffmann, Yoel. (Tr.) *Every End Exposed—The 100 Perfect Koans of Master Kido.* Brookline, Massachusetts: Autumn Press, 1977

Izutsu, Toshihiko. *Towards a Philosophy of Zen Buddhism.* Boulder,

Colorado: Great Eastern Book Co., 1982.

Johnson, Robert A. *Owning Your Own Shadow: Understanding the Dark Side of the Psyche.* San Francisco: Harper Collins, 1991.

Kurtz, Ernest and Katherine Ketcham. *The Spirituality of Imperfection: Storytelling and the Journey to Wholeness.* New York: Bantam Books, 1994.

Lu K'uan Yu, Charles. *Ch'an and Zen Teaching.* York Beach. Me.: Samuel Weiser Inc, 1993.

Narasimha Swami, B.V. *Self-realization: Life and Teachings of Sri Ramana Maharishi.* Thiruvannamalai, Sri Ramanasramam, 1968.

Oldenberg, Hermann. *Buddha: His Life, His Doctrine, His Order.* Tr. from the German by William Hoey. Calcutta: Calcutta Book Company. 1927.

Reps, Paul. *Zen Flesh, Zen Bones.* Boston & London: Shambhala Publications,1994.

Scharlemann, Robert P. *The Reason of Following.* Chicago and London: University of Chicago Press, 1991.

Sekida, Katsuki. *Two Zen Classics—Mumonkan and Hekiganroku.* New York: Weatherhill, 1977.

Shibayama, Zenkei. *Zen Comments on the Mumonkan.* New York: Harper and Row, 1974.

Sung, Bae Park. *Buddhist Faith and Sudden Enlightenment.* New Delhi: Motilal Banarsidas, 1983.

Suzuki, D.T. *Essays in Zen Buddhism—First Series.* New Delhi: Munshiram Manoharlal Publishers Pvt Ltd, 2000.

The Collected Works of Sri Ramana Maharishi.
Thiruvannamalai, Sri Ramanasramam

Walsh, David. *Guarded by Mystery: Meaning in a Postmodern Age.* Washington D.C: The Catholic University of America Press, 1999.

Watson, Burton. (Tr.) *The Zen Teachings of Master Lin-Chi by I. Hsuan.* Boston & London: Shambhala Publications, 1993.

Wilber, Ken. *One Taste: Daily Reflections on Integral Spirituality.* Boston & London: Shambhala Publications, 1999.

Yamada Ko-Un. *Gateless Gate.* Los Angeles: Center Publications, 1979.